Counting the Cost

Raising and Coaching Elite Athletes

Richard Fowler, Stacy Hall, and Holly Haynes

Counting the Cost: Raising and Coaching Elite Athletes / Richard Fowler, Stacy Hall, and Holly Haynes
ISBN: 978-1-95402-205-8
First Printing: 2025, TMU Press, Cleveland, Georgia

Truett McConnell
University

Contents

Foreword

Counting the Cost is a book filled with common sense that has been grounded in research and practical insights. But we know that so often common sense is not practiced and understood. *Counting the Cost* is easy to understand and easy to put into practice in the way principles, strategies, and frankly common sense are laid out throughout the book.

Whether you are an athlete, parent/caregiver, or coach, *Counting the Cost* gives principles and advice that will help a young athlete not only to perform at a higher athletic level but also to excel in life far beyond athletics.

Counting the Cost addresses every aspect of sports from the physical, emotional, mental, and even financial factors that need to be thought through in pursing athletics and life beyond athletics. While reading I kept thinking of parents, athletes, and coaches from elementary to professional athletic levels who would benefit from reading this book. I will definitely be giving *Counting the Cost* to athletes, parents, and coaches at every level of sports whom I know will benefit from not only reading it but continually referencing it to excel not only in sports but in every area of life.

Through the years serving as the chaplain for the Atlanta Braves Organization, I have sat in the conference room in the Atlanta Braves front office and heard many conversations from executives and players about young athletes, their parents and coaches, and the unhealthy and unbalanced approach that many of them put on achieving success in athletics at any cost. *Counting the Cost* gives a healthy and balanced approach to helping young athletes, their parents, and coaches develop a healthy and balanced approach to sports physically, mentally, and emotionally. This healthy balance presented in *Counting the Cost* will help young athletes succeed not only on the field of play but in life.

Jay McSwain
President & Founder, PLACE Ministries

Introduction

Rick Fowler

Most parents think that their children are the most talented, most intelligent, and most likeable human beings on the planet. Even though this conclusion represents, for the most part, a biased perspective, when it comes to sport participation, many caregivers don't stop to evaluate the reality of their presuppositions and the total cost it takes to raise a star elite athlete.

The authors of this book, however, desire to paint a realistic picture by providing an honest look at the components necessary for one to become a star athlete. The Bible, in Luke 14:28-31 (NASB), gives two great principles for parents to first consider before entering their potential "prodigy" into the fast-paced, pressure-packed world of athletics, a journey that can last for twenty plus years:

> For which of you, who wants to build a tower, does not first sit down and calculate the cost, to see if he has enough to complete it? Otherwise, when he has laid a foundation, and is not able to finish, all who observe it begin to ridicule him saying, "This man began to build, and was not able to finish." Or, what king, when he has set out to meet another king in battle, will not first sit down and take counsel whether he is strong enough with ten thousand men to encounter the one coming against him with twenty thousand?

Two principles can be gleaned from this Bible passage. First, caregivers ought not to make a rash commitment to place their child on the track that may or may not arrive at the destination called "elite athleticism" without understanding and obligating themselves to teaching the five essential points of a star, which encompass the development of the emotional, mental, physical, and moral elements of the young athlete, along with their financial involvement to make it happen. Second, like the king in the last portion of this passage who needed reassurance that the soldiers he had could win the battle, parents also need non-biased evaluations of their children's abilities before engaging them in a situation that would provide great benefits or great sorrow.

Counting the Cost: Raising & Coaching Elite Athletes is a template that will help caregivers see a holistic view of the necessary ingredients involved for a player to become known as an "elite athlete." Becoming a star athlete, then, is a symphony production composed of parents, coaches, and athletes all coming together to produce a harmonious product that is enjoyed and admired by all.

CHAPTER ONE

Worldview and the Athlete

Richard Fowler, Stacy Hall, and Holly Haynes

Worldviews . . . are like the foundations of a house: vital, but invisible. They are that through which, not at which, a society or an individual normally looks; they form the grid according to which humans organize reality, not bits of reality that offer themselves for organization.
—N. T. Wright, *The New Testament and the People of God*

Many times, I've observed individuals, including myself (Stacy), navigating through life, making a plethora of decisions that profoundly impact their lives. These choices often appear to be driven by immediate self-interest, lacking a coherent plan, an overarching purpose, or a clear direction. Some decisions may be seemingly inconsequential, like how to spend time with friends or which movie to watch. In contrast, others are of paramount significance, such as choosing a life partner, deciding when to start a family, shaping a professional career, and managing finances, among others. These choices might be swayed by the prevailing societal norms. Regrettably, when these decisions are made in isolation, they tend to lack cohesion, synergy, and alignment with core values. Furthermore, societal norms can be as fickle as the wind, providing no enduring reference point for truth, morality, or righteousness. So, what can serve as the bedrock for our values, guide our decision-making, and foster coherence in our lives?

Defining Worldview

A worldview acts as the lens through which we perceive the world around us. This concept was first introduced by the 19th-century philosopher Immanuel Kant. According to Kant (1797), a worldview is the framework that shapes how we interpret our interactions with the world. It answers questions about our existence, purpose in life, self-worth, how we treat others, and how we respond to both positive and negative events. It influences our thoughts, behavior, actions, and even our motivation. A well-defined worldview can be the driving force that propels us out of bed each morning or the factor that keeps us in slumber. It can either lead us to live a fulfilling and meaningful life or confine us to a passive existence where others determine our destiny. Our worldview is shaped and filtered by the various stimuli we encounter throughout our lives.

Worldview is a multifaceted construct influenced by culture, family, geographical location, historical era, and personal beliefs. For instance, individuals may hold diverse perspectives on the purpose of life. Some may believe life is a result of mere chance, a series of coincidental and random events with no divine authorship, no ultimate destination, only the present moment. In such a worldview, our purpose might be reduced to the cultivation and utilization of our survival instincts.

A worldview acts as the lens through which we perceive the world. It's the filter through which we interpret our interactions, determine our purpose, assess our self-worth, guide our interactions with others, and shape our responses to life's challenges. It can motivate us to act, set the tone for our day, and provide a foundation for ethical decision-making.

With this worldview as our guiding filter, our thoughts and behaviors may significantly differ from those adhering to a religious or alternative worldview. As proponents of a Biblical worldview, we offer a distinct perspective on life's purpose. Serving as the ultimate guide for the Christian worldview, the Bible asserts that we are "made in the image of God" (Genesis 1:28), "fearfully and wonderfully made" (Psalm 139:14), and "called according to His purpose" (Romans 8:28). Christians believe that they are unique creations of a loving God, each with a predetermined purpose established long before birth. A Christian worldview acknowledges that God is the ultimate author of existence, and everything is intricately designed. It leaves no room for accidents or happenstances. Simultaneously, it recognizes human imperfection and the need for the Savior. Therefore, Christians are called to conduct their thoughts and actions as if they are serving the Lord, which imparts a higher purpose to their lives.

This profound understanding of the world and our place in it influences our behavior and interactions with others. Whether you're an athlete, coach, or parent of an elite athlete, your worldview shapes your responses to the various challenges within the several aspects of a star athlete: physical, emotional, and mental.

In essence, becoming an elite athlete demands a significant investment, not only physically but also emotionally, mentally (in terms of discipline), and morally. Your worldview helps you prioritize what truly matters in this journey.

Worldview and Elite Athletes: A Model

In the realm of physicality, worldview profoundly impacts athletic talent. It fosters an understanding that our talents and abilities are divine gifts, encouraging us to make the most of them as a form of service to God. This perspective extends to our relationships with parents, coaches, teammates, officials, and competitors, emphasizing that our talents are meant to be used to the best of our abilities.

Emotionally, worldview provides a profound sense of peace and self-understanding. For Texas Hall of Fame honoree Coach Gary A. Moore (who holds the record as the "All Time Winningest Coach" in Texas high school football), it is a reminder that our identity is not solely defined by our athletic prowess. We are first and foremost creations of God, called to worship and fulfill a higher purpose. Our self-worth is not tethered to our sports performance but rests securely in God's love and grace. Sports are not our sole identity; they are an avenue through which we can use our gifts to glorify our Creator. (personal interview conducted by Corbitt Howard, February 3, 2023)

Moral code is another dimension significantly shaped by one's worldview. It involves a consistent set of moral principles that guide our behavior. Our worldview can substantially impact the extent to which we are disciplined in our actions, adhering to our beliefs about right and wrong. Elite athletes must possess inherent self-discipline, dedicating the time required for high-level competition and elite performance. Your moral code shapes your ability to stay on track.

Your worldview acts as a filter, coloring your perspectives and influencing every facet of your life. It serves as the psychological DNA that defines you. Just as a tree's roots and soil composition influence its growth, your worldview profoundly shapes who you are and how you navigate the world.

When coaches assemble their athletes, they often only see the outward manifestations of their players. They may have limited understanding of the deeper dimensions of an athlete's makeup. In cases where coaches oversee large teams, like football teams with over a hundred players, it can be nearly impossible to delve into the nuances of each athlete's worldview without the assistance of other staff members, as we will discuss later.

Understanding how a worldview influences an athlete provides valuable insights into the unique traits and behaviors that set athletes apart. When trying to understand the complex influence of a worldview, coaches and caregivers often ask four questions:

1. Why does one athlete "freeze" in a close game and a peer does not?

2. What makes one athlete lose control when the referee makes a bad call, while others can keep his/her composure?

3.   What makes an athlete seek out and enjoy the pressure of a crucial last shot or penalty kick, while a fellow player shies away from that challenge?

4.   Why are some athletes passionate about practice (often arriving early or leaving late) when others arrive just seconds before practice and are the first to leave when the official practice is over?

The answer to these questions can be summed up in a single word: worldview. The worldview of an athlete, whether conscious or unconscious, permeates every aspect of their performance. That's why we place "worldview" as one of the points of the star. The other dimensions discussed in this book (physicality, emotional response, and mental awareness) are all filtered through and determined by an athlete's worldview. In today's sports landscape, the psychological and environmental components are the "X" factors that differentiate it from the sports culture of four decades ago. Since understanding what motivates a player is often the key to success, many sports programs now employ sports psychologists.

For sports teams to thrive and for athletes to reach their full potential, coaches must make an extra effort to truly understand their players. This deeper level of understanding allows coaches to respond in ways that have a more positive and lasting impact.

A worldview for any individual is multifaceted and complex. Parts of this complexity hinge on environmental factors that must be pinpointed and evaluated to truly understand the potential quality of an athlete.

Environmental Factors Affecting Worldview

Temperament of the Athlete
Coaches need to start the analysis of their players by determining their primary motivating force. How athletes define their purpose can predict how they will perform in an athletic contest. In most cases, temperament can be classified into four groups:

1.   **Personal Affirmation**: If this motivational component is ignored, the player will feel his/her worth is

minimized and so will tend to underperform. This player may desire to win and play well, but the primary reward for them is affirmation.

2. **Analytical Thinking and Ideas**: This player needs to be allowed to share ideas about the team, the plays, and team issues at appropriate times without being judged as a troublemaker.

3. **Consistency**: Routine is the lifeblood of this athlete. He/she may have a difficult time operating outside of the box and will feel threatened when asked to be spontaneous. For this player to become an elite athlete, coaches may need to provide not only team routines, but also spontaneous activities to allow the player to become more mentally relaxed in such a setting.

4. **Task Completion**: To team peers, this type of athlete may seem "arrogant" or even "bullish" at times. These players are the no-nonsense players and often work to keep the team on track. Coaches can delegate the role of "captain" to these athletes who gain a sense of accomplishment from carrying out their wishes on the field.

For a team to be successful, all four types are needed. No team functions well with only captains on the field. Each type of player has his/her strong points to contribute to the well-being of the team. And any of these types can be the foundation for the creation of an elite athlete if the coach places that individual in the right position with the right team dynamics. Examples of players not being used according to their psychological bent on the team can be found in nearly every sport. However, when those same players are traded to another team and given the opportunity to play according to their temperaments, they become all-pro athletes.

The Athlete's Family of Origin

An individual's family of origin of course plays a major role in worldview development. For example, if a child is generally enabled or overprotected and not forced to deal with conflict, that person will filter this through his or her worldview as the way the world works and will take that attitude into the arena of play. On the flipside, if a child is raised with more of a "no pain, no gain" philosophy, he or she will take that kind of a worldview into the sports arena.

An area of concern, however, is the sad reality that many youngsters today are raised in a single-parent, or even no-parent, home. They are left without guidance or protection of those positive values which could provide the necessary framework to become an elite athlete. Helping an individual in today's culture become an elite player often requires a caring, loving coach who is willing to take on a mother or father role that will inculcate lasting values and goals.

The Athlete's Societal Influence

Societal influences without doubt also influence the worldview of an athlete. It is easy to see that an athlete raised in Brazil would most likely embrace soccer instead of American football and grow up idolizing the greatest soccer player of all time, Pele. In urban areas of America, where outdoor hoops and pick up ball often fills the vacant hours of a child's life, athletes will more likely adopt a worldview which idolizes Michael Jordan or Stephen Curry.

The Physical Constraints of the Athlete

Finally, the physical makeup of an individual influences but does not totally dictate one's worldview. If a male athlete is 5'8, and loves basketball, he is not going to aspire to play as a center. Instead, this player will naturally focus on developing the skills to become a great point guard because his physique more or less dictates this, and his worldview then aligns with this set of "givens."

Obviously, there are exceptions to this point. We all know or have heard of an athlete who overcame a physical limitation that would have sidelined others. In these cases, temperament and/or family of origin values have trumped physical limitations.

Summary

It may seem like a person's worldview is something that is learned through osmosis and can be fatalistic. However, athletes can still choose to fight against negative influences and defy the odds, much like a salmon can swim upstream to spawn or a bumble bee can fly despite the laws of physics. There are numerous examples of athletic success that have been achieved through a change in worldview or a rejection of the "typical" worldview. For instance, Wayne Gretzky and Jerry Rice were both deemed unfit for their respective sports, but they went on to become some of the greatest players in history. A documentary titled, *In Search of Greatness* (2018), provides a glimpse into their stories.

To consistently win and succeed at an elite level, coaches must now understand how one's worldview affects performance. Too often, people make decisions based solely on their own benefit without any real plan or direction. While some decisions may be trivial, others have a significant impact on one's life, such as choosing a life partner, starting a family, selecting a career path, and managing finances. These decisions can be influenced by societal norms, which can change frequently and provide no true reference point for values, morality, or righteousness. It is therefore important to find an anchor for our values, align our decision-making, and provide cohesion in our lives.

Choices seem best when anchored in core values. As coaches assemble teams, they see outward manifestations, not internal drivers. Understanding worldview provides insights to shape positive coaching. Athletes perform best when worldviews align with training. Coaching "according to an athlete's bent" (Proverbs 22:6) elicits lasting growth. The coach's assessment should reveal player temperaments for ideal training. Winning flows from cohesion between worldview and coaching approach.

To better understand the "givens" of an athlete, coaches can go to the companion of this book, "A Coach's Toolbox of Assessments," to administer the "Coaching Preference Profile."

CHAPTER TWO

The Athlete and Physical Cost

Holly Haynes

I been grindin' all day and all night
Hall of fame, on my mind
Tryna be the greatest, of all time
And say it's all God, that's all
I been grindin' all day and all night
Hall of fame, on my mind
Tryna be the greatest, of all time
Then say it's all God, that's all
I been grinding all-
—Swoope, "Hall of Fame"

When we look at the cost of greatness, the most recognizable cost is often physical. Our nation is fascinated by the documentaries and films that show athletes "grindin' all day and all night" like *Rocky, Chariots of Fire, Rudy, Remember the Titans,* and *The Blindside* (Swoope, "Hall of Fame"). These stories speak to sacrifice—often physical—to meet lofty athletic goals. Many will put their bodies on the line for long-term glory. However, when we look at the physical cost for the elite athlete, there are several variables that must be counted. One of the most important of those variables is practice—the grind. How and why we practice as elite athletes are key to overall athletic success.

The 10,000-Hour Rule

Every athlete is required to practice their sport to improve. In fact, success in most fields is tied to a commitment to regular and consistent practice. Students stay after school to practice with their teammates so that they learn to run plays, build trust, and improve skills. Club sports often require a 3-4 day-a-week team practice schedule. Individual sports are no different from team sports in requirements for practice; golfers, figure skaters, and tennis players (among others) spend ample time in gyms and on the field perfecting shots and turns.

Today, practice and athletes have been influenced by Malcolm Gladwell's (2008) popularization of the "10,000-Hour Rule" through his book *Outliers: The Story of Success*. According to Gladwell, a 1993 study of elite musicians demonstrated that "deliberate practice" separated the top 1% of musicians from the other equally talented musicians (as cited in Ericsson et al., 1993). Gladwell then elicited from the study that this deliberate practice required a certain amount of time—10,000 hours to be exact. So, those who rose to the very top of an equally talented group of musicians spent more time in deliberate practice than others. Gladwell went on in his book to generalize the findings to successful pilots, rock bands, athletes, and even computer scientists, such as Bill Gates and Steve Jobs.

Researchers set out to replicate the work. Over the past years, research on the "10,000-Hour Rule" has shown mixed results. Interestingly, much of the research has been conducted on musicians (Ericsson & Harwell, 2019). Some studies suggest that practicing for 10,000 hours makes one an expert. Other studies' results suggest no significant impact of 10,000 hours of practice. So, where does it lie with athletes? According to current research, the "10,000-Hour Rule" is key for elite athletes (Ko, 2021). However, the type of practice needed for athletes to be successful is a very specific type of practice—deliberate practice. Ko suggests that deliberate practice is a critical component of athletic success.

It makes sense that deliberate practice can lead to athletic success. It also makes sense that it takes about 10,000 hours to become an "expert" in a task. When *Outliers* was published in 2008, coaches, teachers, instructors, and parents took the 10,000 hours literally. [In fact, as a parent, it validated all the hours of waiting and the miles driven to practices.] It also validated all the money spent on private training. However, for athletes, deliberate practice alone—even 10,000 hours—is not going to equal success. It is just one component of what it takes to be an elite athlete.

Deliberate practice must be combined with a worldview for athletes to be successful at their craft. Many elite athletes realize that there are others striving towards similar goals: the professional contract, the college scholarship, or the Olympic medal. They also appear to understand that practice is required to keep themselves a step ahead of other athletes. My older two children often say that their mentality/worldview about practice is not the same as their younger brother's. For them, practice is just a necessary element to keep them fit. They dread going, but they know it is a requirement for them to achieve some success in their sport. Their worldview is about the here and now. When discussing their brother, they say, "He is different. He actually likes to practice." But that is not correct. Their little brother sees the grind—practice—as a means to an end. In his mind, if he is to maintain and improve his skills, he must put in time away from his teammates on his own. Biographies of elite athletes demonstrate this similar practice mentality. The Williams sisters practiced late into the night to perfect their serve. Lionel Messi speaks of always having a ball at his feet—indoors and outdoors. Pele used mangoes to train and develop a brilliant touch while completing housework. Deliberate practice plus an elite mindset/worldview often means that elite athletes put in 10,000 hours long before their own teammates and other athletes of the same age. However, practice is not just a task they must do because they were told to do so. Practice is a necessary means to an end.

Work Smarter, Not Harder

As stated above, parents were delighted by the idea of deliberate practice. Parents have been encouraging their children to practice for generations. We teach children to practice times tables, the piano, and manners. However, deliberate practice is only one component of success. How many times have you seen a teammate who puts in all the private practice but performs poorly in the actual game? In fact, the parents may be driving that player to multiple trainers during the week. Why is this teammate seemingly less successful than others who train at the same level? It may be because there are more components to practice than just repetition.

You may have heard the phrase, "work smarter, not harder." We can apply this to our sports, our schoolwork, or our careers. Our society often just focuses on working hard. And, yes, hard work is important, but smart work is much more valuable. For athletes, media (e.g., music, YouTube, TikTok) often encourages an expectation to work out constantly. Trainers post workouts for players on Instagram. Athletes post videos of themselves completing various training tasks. It would appear that if you are not working hard—not grindin' all day and all night—that you could lose your spot or position to another athlete.

However, what research shows is that practicing smarter is critical to the improvement of athletic skills, and it is what sets apart the elite athlete. Chow et al. (2019) posit that the acquisition of a specific skill is enhanced by "specific practice." Essentially, rather than go through a series of skills that may be transferable to game time, practice specific skills and relate them to game time simulations during practice. And, while it may seem like it is the coach's responsibility to set up a training session that utilizes "specific practice" or "deliberate practice," it is also the player's responsibility to think about how specific drills relate to their performance in game situations (Woods et al., 2020). So, practice is not only about building muscle memory; it is most helpful when athletes begin to apply/think about what they are learning to their performance on the field.

There are additional ways of working smarter and not harder. Sometimes, we need to be more creative in practice. Galatti et al. (2019) found that elite female basketball players in Brazil spent time in their youth practicing on their own and practicing in varied settings.

I'll give you a short example. My older son was cut from a soccer club because he was physically shorter than children his same age. In fact, he was not going to gain much height because he was going to move through puberty at a later stage than his peers. Although this was mentally devasting news, it forced him to rethink how and where he practiced. He went back to his former club, but it was not his 4 day a week practice that helped him improve his skills. Those practices focused on teamwork and game day strategy. There was very little attention to some of the elements he needed to focus on as a smaller player on the field. Where could he develop strategies for playing against older, more developed players? The answer was just around the corner at our local park.

My then 13-year-old son took ownership of his athletic growth and started playing pickup soccer with adult men in the park. I know. It sounds a little dangerous, and at first, I was concerned about injury. However, what we know about elite athletes is that their mind is set to take on challenges. They also seek opportunities to improve—especially in areas of weakness. For my son, unstructured, creative play helped improve his technical skills, his mental toughness, and his creativity on the field. Playing against men made him less fearful of larger opponents. This style of practice, while uncommon and unsupported by many clubs, is the practice style of children around the world who play soccer and basketball. And, this style has been found to be critical in the development of elite athletes in both of those sports (Roca & Ford, 2021).

Playing in unstructured environments often teaches more skills and encourages more creativity. By the way, through these pickup games, he also gained those 10,000 hours of deliberate practice. Sometimes athletes need to move away from what they normally do in a practice session (team or private) and focus on creative ways of improving their skills. Football players may take dance lessons. Basketball players may play in 3v3 tournaments. It may not look like practice, but it often better supports player development.

Understanding and Using Physical Limitations

I mentioned earlier that my son was smaller in size than his fellow athletes. That specifically related to his height as he moved into puberty. Our youngest son is also smaller than his peers and will probably follow a similar delayed puberty path. Knowing that our youngest has professional goals and aspirations, my husband and I were very concerned about how to manage his physical limitations, especially as his peers approached puberty. You see, sport and size often go hand in hand. Yet, there are always exceptions to the rule. Steph Curry, Russell Wilson, and Lionel Messi are all "too short" for their sports. Tom Brady's times in his NFL combine tryout were defined by his lack of athleticism. So, what do you do with your physical limitations?

First, we must acknowledge that they exist. Then, you must use those limitations to your advantage. Sometimes, we choose sports because of our height. My husband and I chose to place our children into soccer because there are several players of average height. But, in general, our perception is that athletes are bigger, faster, and stronger than the average competitor. David Epstein, author of *The Sports Gene: Inside the Science of Extraordinary Athletic Performance* (2014), suggests that we use "specialized bodies" in modern athletics. What this means is that coaches select particular body types for particular sports. So, yes, modern athletes are bigger, faster, and stronger, but it varies based on the sport. Additionally, Epstein argues that modern technologies and changes in techniques have shifted the nature of the sport. He suggests that what is very important in understanding the relationship between size and athletics is that multiple factors determine success in each sport. And, while size and speed are definitely factors, understanding a given size and using it to one's advantage is even more important.

Using size to your advantage can be difficult, but the concept of *proprioception* can be useful here. *Proprioception*, simply put, is an unconscious, heightened awareness of one's body. In many ways, elite athletes who understand their bodies can physically outperform others because their bodies and minds are in a unique synchronicity. However, what is key in understanding the benefit of proprioception is that athletes understand their bodies and are comfortable in understanding their strengths and limitations. They use these strengths to their advantage. Let me provide a few examples.

A few years ago, I was conversing with one of our exceptionally tall collegiate basketball players about smaller players on the court—the 5'10 and 6' athletes. Considering that this player was 7' tall, I thought that he would discuss the advantage of rebounding and slam dunking over the heads of the more diminutive basketball player. Surprisingly, he told me that he hated playing against small players. He said that he couldn't see them. I was stunned, so I asked him to explain. He stated that smaller players tend to be quicker. The smaller player forced him to change the way he played because rather than play standing tall, he had to hunch over to see the player. Basically, small players threw off his proprioception.

In contrast, our daughter is a diminutive soccer player. She is all of 5 ft 1 in. However, she played much of her soccer career in a position that is regularly reserved for girls who are 5'7" and taller. Playing in this position meant that she faced girls who were often much taller; coaches often played their tallest or largest player against her. She was quite successful in her position. Her team often had one of the lowest goals scored against averages in the league. How did she do it? When she was a child, she earned a black belt in taekwondo. During that time, she competed in several tournaments where she was the lightest in her weight class. What she learned to do at the competitions was to use her small size and quickness to beat her heavier opponents. She transferred that skill to the soccer field. She would make herself smaller than her taller opponents. As the basketball player above told us—tall players can't see smaller players coming. It throws off their perception. And, that is what she did. She learned to be very quiet, to roll herself into a ball, and steal the ball away from her opponent with quickness.

I will say that while she secured quite a bit of success on the field and used her flexibility, vision, and insight in creative ways, many coaches overlooked her initially when she said that she played the position. We will take this up later in the book as we look at coaching and physical cost. Elite athletes must learn to understand, accept, and utilize their physical strengths and limitations.

As I write this chapter, my youngest is facing off, completing 1v1s with his older brother in a small room in our house. He is facing an opponent who is more than 1 foot taller and outweighs him by 60 pounds in close quarters. Yet, there they are—facing off time and time again as my youngest is challenged to use his skill, touch, and creativity to get a ball past what seems like a giant. He fails a lot, but he also gets that ball through his brother's legs and around him a lot.

This scene is a microcosm of the challenges and growth opportunities we've discussed throughout this chapter. It embodies the concepts of deliberate practice, working smarter, and using physical limitations to one's advantage. The confined space and the significant size difference between the brothers create a crucible for skill development that goes beyond what might be achieved in a more traditional practice setting.

By the way, this scenario often leads to the success of the youngest child in a family (Williams & Wigmore, 2020). Wayne Gretzky, Serena Williams, and Michael Jordan are all younger siblings whose older siblings played the same sport. This phenomenon happens because younger siblings are engaged in deliberate and creative practice with their older siblings. Additionally, they are playing against faster and stronger athletes, so they develop mentally, technically, and physically.

This observation about younger siblings in athletic families is fascinating and provides insight into how challenging environments can foster exceptional talent. The constant exposure to more advanced competition forces these younger siblings to adapt, innovate, and excel in ways that their peers might not experience. It's a form of "specific practice" that occurs naturally within the family dynamic.

The examples of Gretzky, Williams, and Jordan are particularly powerful. These athletes, considered among the greatest in their respective sports, all benefited from this unique family dynamic. It suggests that the combination of sibling rivalry, constant access to a more advanced practice partner, and the need to overcome physical disadvantages can be a potent recipe for athletic success.

If athletes learn to be comfortable with their size and determine how to use it to their advantage, the sky is the limit. This mindset—embracing one's physical attributes, whether they're perceived as advantages or limitations—is perhaps the most crucial lesson for aspiring elite athletes. It's not about trying to fit into a predetermined mold of what an athlete in a particular sport should look like. Instead, it's about understanding your unique physical tools and leveraging them to maximum effect.

This approach requires creativity, resilience, and a willingness to think outside the box. It might mean developing unconventional techniques, like my daughter's soccer strategy, or finding innovative ways to practice, like my son's pickup games with adults. It's about turning perceived weaknesses into strengths and challenging the status quo of what's possible in a given sport.

Ultimately, the physical cost of greatness isn't just about the hours spent in practice or the toll taken on the body. It's about the mental fortitude required to approach practice intelligently, to face challenges head-on, and to constantly seek ways to improve. It's about understanding that physical limitations are often just opportunities in disguise, waiting for the right mindset and approach to transform them into unique advantages.

As we've seen throughout this chapter, becoming an elite athlete is a complex journey that goes far beyond simply putting in the hours. It requires deliberate, thoughtful practice, a willingness to seek out challenging situations, and the creativity to turn physical realities into competitive advantages. For those willing to embrace this approach, the potential for athletic achievement is limitless.

CHAPTER THREE

The Coach and Physical Cost

Richard Fowler, Stacy Hall, and Holly Haynes

> *Feel the rain on your skin*
> *No one else can feel it for you*
> *Only you can let it in*
> *No one else, no one else*
> *Can speak the words on your lips*
> *Drench yourself in words unspoken*
> *Live your life with arms wide open*
> *Today is where your book begins*
> *The rest is still unwritten.*
> —Natasha Bedingfield, "Unwritten"

Sizing Them Up: Understanding Athlete Physiology and Growth

America's Obsession with Size and Speed

Size matters. Well, according to many coaches, size is the very first thing assessed before welcoming a player onto a team. Although size is not everything, physicality has its place in sports.

There is not a single coach that does not look at a nine-year-old that is gifted with height or weight and attempt to place that child on their American football or basketball team. We know that parents often attempt to find the right sport for their child based on their size and speed. Coaches set the tempo for this as well. My daughter tried out for a statewide soccer team. They call it the Olympic Development Program. Now, as I mentioned in a previous chapter, she plays a position that is often reserved for tall players. She is diminutive at best. However, one thing I did not mention is that she is a very strong player. Additionally, she is very flexible. When she went to the tryout, she told the coach that she usually played the center back position. At that moment, he sized her up and determined that she would not make the team—even before she set foot on the field. He apologized to her after the tryout—admitting that he did not believe that she could play the position. Throughout the season, she would become his most trusted player on the field.

But was the coach wrong? If we review the literature, we find that athletes have been getting taller, faster, and stronger (McClusky, 2014). Coaches perceive this, but at the younger levels, do we push children out of sports who could become elite athletes because of our bias towards exceptional physicality? An understanding of human growth and development may help us better understand and accommodate all elite athletes, regardless of size.

Human Growth and Development as Related to Athletes

The growth of the field of exercise science has been helpful to many training programs from elite soccer academies to collegiate and professional programs. However, the science of exercise and sport should not replace the study of growth and development from a psychological perspective. Human growth and development also encompasses brain development and can help coaches better understand everything from growth spurts to attitude to mood in elite athletes. Human growth and development combines physiology with psychology. A good understanding of it can help coaches better design the practices discussed later in the chapter.

Coaches, Train Smarter, Not Harder

I first heard the term, "Train smarter rather than harder" when I was in the early stage of my flight training. I was learning how to appropriately take off by pulling the yoke back to gain lift. There was a lot of pressure on the yoke making it seem like isometric exercise. The next time I took off, however, my instructor said to me, "You can fly smarter rather than harder by adjusting the trim tab in order to gain altitude without having to pull hard on the yoke, making your takeoff easy." In various ways, this is a metaphor for how coaches need to train their elite athletes.

In this section, we will present ten concepts and strategies that can enable coaches to train their elite athletes smarter, in ways that will obtain the best results.

Understanding Current Culture

To obtain the best results when training elite athletes, coaches need to understand the culture of the players that they are investing in. To most effectively train elite athletes, coaches should look for connections that go beyond the "x's and o's." In fact, today's cultural environment demands that a greater percentage of the coach's time and skills be spent apart from the field or court and away from the locker room. The primary reason can be attributed to a shift in how youngsters are taught to view themselves and their abilities.

In the late 1800's, a German sociologist, Ferdinand Tönnies (2001), coined the words, *Gemeinschaft* and *Gesellschaft* to describe two types of communities. *Gemeinschaft* was defined as a community/society that worked together for the good of all, based on common values and beliefs. In contrast, *Gesellschaft* was defined as a society that based its interactions solely on how the community could be used to enhance personal goals. If Tönnies were alive today, he would say athletes have shifted from a *Gemeinschaft* to a *Gesellschaft* setting. Many youngsters have been taught to focus more on their individual accolades and ambitions regardless of how it affects their team instead of focusing on team achievements. Many in this generation have been raised to believe that everyone should get a trophy. Paying one's dues to earn a starting spot is archaic at best.

Many elite athletes see themselves as set apart from the rest of the team because their environmental circle has confirmed this to them. Therefore, it is often the elite athlete who will hold the team hostage. Sadly, it is now so common to hear comments like, "If I don't get my way, I will put my name in the transfer portal" (i.e., NIL rules for NCAA athletes).

Therefore, coaching elite athletes may require a backdoor approach in dealing with this cultural dimension. There is an old saying that says, "You can lead a horse to water, but you can't make him drink." That may be true, but there is nothing to prohibit us from putting out a salt block or two for the horse to lick, which in turn makes it thirsty enough to go to the water tank and drink. In the same way, coaching elite athletes does not require a dismissal of team discipline or team objectives, but it does require coaches to put out training "salt blocks" (that adjusts to the current culture of the athletes) so the end result will not be compromised. The coaching philosophy of many, "my way or the highway," often won't work with today's elite athletes.

AP sportswriter, Janie McCauley (2022), summed it up this way:

> Sports programs across the county are weighing whether such tough coaching styles have a place in a world where student-athletes demand more sensitive treatment and more individualized training. Athletes of this younger generation wield greater personal power over their career

paths, which can force coaches to accommodate them or risk losing top talent.

This observation highlights a fundamental shift in the coach-athlete dynamic. Where coaches once held nearly absolute authority, today's athletes expect—and often demand—a more collaborative relationship. This change reflects broader societal shifts toward recognizing individual autonomy and mental health needs.

The challenge for modern coaches lies in finding the right balance between maintaining necessary discipline and adapting to evolving expectations. Many successful coaches have discovered that modifying their approach doesn't mean compromising standards—rather, it means finding new ways to motivate and develop athletes that align with contemporary values while still achieving excellence.

Elevate; Don't Exasperate

Over the years of observing coaches, I have witnessed many who carry the slogan "We must be tough to get our players to play tough." To some, this means demeaning any perceived weakness or shortcoming. These coaches seem to believe that an emphasis on encouragement weakens intense performance. Built into the athlete/coach relationship is a unique power to build up or tear down. Colossians 3:21 (NASB) says, "Fathers [or coaches], do not exasperate your child [or players], so that they do not lose heart." The word *exasperate* means "to irritate intensely, provoke anger, or stir up feelings of resentment and discouragement." The purpose of this prohibition is to prevent the child (athlete) from losing heart. If a coach stirs up an athlete's anger, the result often is not better performance, but rather discouragement. And in some cases, it will cause that player to quit altogether. If coaches/parents understand and utilize a simple formula called the 5-1 ratio, there will be much less exasperation and way more encouragement for life and sports. Basically, this formula says, "for every one instructive comment, follow that up with five affirming comments" like "Keep it up" or "You got this." This is the philosophy of sports advocate Tony Cammarota, who set forth several ways to exasperate athletes and their remedies (2016). We will address three.

First, coaches ought not demand something the athlete cannot accomplish. We should not set unreasonable goals or place excessive pressure on a player to perform. It is quite common for coaches to expect too much from their elite athletes. Such was the case with Art. Art was 6'4 in the sixth grade and 6'7 by the 9th grade. Because of his size and natural talent, coaches looked at him as if they had won the lottery. However, Art had learning differences that put him on a slower track toward maturity. The 5-1 ratio may have given him the encouragement to become truly outstanding. But the coaching he experienced caused him to quit basketball for good after his sophomore year in college. Coaches need to be clear of their expectations, to understand their athletes as best they can, and to set appropriate goals—goals that focus on character development, sportsmanship, and attitude. It was reported that all-time great, Coach John Wooden of UCLA, following every game asked each player, "Did you play up to your potential tonight?" This gives the player a valuable chance at self-evaluation, rather than simply sitting through a lecture or a teardown.

Second, discouragement is often the result of a coach comparing one player to another. Helping a player grow through instruction is one thing. Making a comparison to another is altogether different, because the athlete will assume the message meant, "I wish you were more like _____." Such tactics set the stage for jealousy and disunity. What's the remedy? Coaches need to keep their comments focused on a particular player, realizing each player has his/her strengths and weaknesses. Teach game fundamentals but be sure to nurture their natural strengths daily.

And third, belittling athletes for their mistakes on a continual basis is always counterproductive. Yelling, scolding, shaming, shouting lectures that beat the player down, have no place in a wise coach's toolbox. Unremitting criticism, nagging, or telling the athlete the same thing over and over will of course have a negative impact on a player. Using words like "never" and "always" are a sure way to discourage. "You never listen to your coach!" and "You always mess up when it counts!" are phrases coaches ought not use. Coaches ought to ask themselves the question, "How do I prefer others respond to me when I fail?" Then simply treat their elite players the way they prefer to be treated. Coaches, do you want your elite players to trust you and desire your coaching? Then let your legacy be that of encouragement.

Elite Players and Positive Reinforcement

If developing athletes are subjected to a predominance of negative stimuli rather than positive reinforcement and instruction, their body systems react in a manner detrimental to the function of vital systems and processes. The most important aspect of sport and athletic training is to ensure that a program is as free from negative factors as possible. The Merriam-Webster dictionary even defines *sport* as: "physical activity engaged in for pleasure" (2009), including synonyms like "play, frolic, fun." Obviously, skill development is not always enjoyable. We are not equating negative reinforcement with simple, hard, and disciplined work.

While visiting a good friend, he asked if I wanted to go jogging with him and a friend the next morning. I agreed before I found out the jogging was to take place at 5 am! Reluctantly, I went, but I am glad I did because I learned a valuable life concept. While jogging I said to the young man we were jogging with, "I understand the need for exercise, but why at 5 am?" He replied simply, "Because I hate it.... I have learned one secret to success is to do something every day that I hate." In this case, "hating to run at 5 am" was not negative reinforcement, but rather it was a motivating factor that enhanced his self-discipline and was a transferable value that affected every area of his life.

The best coaches have learned that positive reinforcement is achieved through the teach-and-train method. Teaching involves the interaction of the psychological along with the cognitive component. Effective coaches teach by keeping players motivated to learn. Sometimes this occurs by answering the simple "How" and "Why" questions. For example, "How will what we are doing make me a better player?" or "Why do we always start and end practice doing _____."

Training on the other hand, is a series of stimuli performed in the attempt to improve the athletes' skill sets by varying between developing strength, speed, coordination, endurance, and the useful concepts of interfacing work, rest, and play. Physical training is positive if properly designed. For developmental training, there must be physical stimuli, recovery, and reapplication. Each level of physical training, however, will produce a certain amount of fatigue. Too little fatigue does not advance a player's skills; too much is harmful (negative reinforcement). The right amount of fatigue is only slightly noticeable, positive, and beneficial.

Gradual Development

The definition of the word *develop* is to "unfold gradually, in detail; to bring out the possibilities of; to acquire gradually" (Merriam-Webster, 2009). The key word is *gradual*, referring to the wisdom in the old saying, "One must learn to crawl before they can walk." There is a very real difference between youth and young adult training and involvement. When young athletes are pushed to peak too early (before their developmental process has been completed), their ability to do so may be impressive. However, in too many cases, their early success brings a very real danger of injury, dropout, burnout, or chronic frustration.

Possibly the greatest loss suffered from accelerated development in the early years is the lack of balance in the athlete's life causing them to become one dimensional. A more beneficial approach is to ensure balanced development: scholastically, socially, and athletically.

Training Core Values

For a player to achieve elite status, the core values of the coach and player must match. If core values are not in sync, the sport maturity of the athlete is halted. Core values are a clear, precise system of beliefs that help people to tell the difference between right and wrong. Core values serve as guiding principles for words and actions, and as markers of identity. Core values drive behavior and form beliefs and facilitate decision making. Thus, everything from practice to games is governed (directly or indirectly) by the core values of the team.

Both coaches and players (if the athlete is a minor, the caregiver) need to identify the core values they desire for themselves and for the team. To get an idea of what a core value might be, coaches and athletes may consider answering the following questions:

- What is your definition of a successful season?
- What are the essential qualities (personal and skill sets) that must exist in order to be labeled a great coach or player?
- What type of relationship ought to exist between a player and a coach?
- What qualities do you admire in your role models?
- What kind of culture do you feel most comfortable working in?
- What motivates you?

More suggestions of core values include adventure, authenticity, bravery, candor, compassion, creativity, dependability, determination, family, fairness, flexibility, honesty, humor, innovation, loyalty, patience, recognition, reliability, respect, responsibility, stability, teamwork, tenacity, transparency, and work ethic.

Too many great players choose a college or a select team because of its reputation or notoriety, or because of a famous coach, when that decision might be the worst choice due to the incompatibility of core values. Coaches would do well to choose players for their teams who agree with their core philosophy of coaching, even if they must pass up a five-star athlete.

The Relationship Between Coaches and Athletes

The relationship coaches have with their elite athletes needs to be measured at three levels. The first level is labeled as a "casual relationship," the second as "a working relationship," and the third as a "bonded relationship."

The *casual relationship* that coaches have with their elite players occurs mostly off-court/field. Players need conversations with their coaches that are not related to business. Relationships are enhanced when players and coaches are relaxed, sharing their lives with each other. It is through casual conversations that mutual trust and understanding are developed.

The *working relationship* occurs mostly during official practice times and at games, when the relationship between coaches and their elite players shifts from a casual context to a more authoritarian interaction. In this setting, the relationship is mostly one-sided (the coach taking the lead) and is focused primarily on business. At this level, coaches initiate information, encouragement, or correction.

The *healthy relational bond* between coach and player should only occur when the athlete is no longer playing under that coach. Many coaches have maintained on-going healthy and appropriate relationships with former players that have proved beneficial and meaningful to both parties. There is an interesting verse in the Bible, found in Luke 6:40 (NASB), which states, "A pupil [or athlete] is not above his teacher [coach]; but everyone, after he has been fully trained [no longer under the tutelage of the coach], will be like [equal] with his teacher [coach]." A word of caution, however. Bonding with athletes, even though healthy, while they are still under the authority of the coach, may lead elite players to arrive at false expectations and feelings of entitlement which will become a detriment to the team as a whole.

Inspiration and the Elite Athlete

The need to be inspired is built into our very own DNA. For example, when the season is waning, often it is the personal inspiration a coach gives that keeps elite players motivated. Counseling an all-pro NFL lineman concerning his increased disinterest in continuing to play, I asked the question, "Isn't making all the millions you get for playing enough to keep you highly motivated?" His answer was quite revealing. "No," he said, "after a while, the money is no longer a motivational factor. What I need and haven't received is for my coaches to inspire me to play harder and better and give me affirmation for the contributions I bring to the team. They think I know when I am doing well, and that by reaching all-pro status, I apparently don't need that affirmation."

On this subject, sports psychologist John O'Sullivan believes that every elite athlete needs three things from a coaching staff: the need for recognition, the need for relevance, and a way to measure a player's contribution (on and off the court or field). The presence of these three things will help the elite player to buy into their program. The absence, or worse, the antithesis, will negatively affect the team and player alike. (O'Sullivan, 2022).

Additionally, coaches need to inspire their star athletes by understanding the temperament of their players. Based on personality, one player may be inspired in one way and a second player in another way. Successful coaches do not coach according to their own personal biases and temperament type; rather, they coach to the bent of the players, since each player is unique and inspired in different ways. A Bible verse that echoes this principle, Proverbs 22:6, states, "Train up a child (athlete) in the way he should go, even when he is old, he will not depart from it" (NASB). The word *train* in the original language of Scripture means to "teach according to the bent of the child (athlete). Effective parenting (or coaching—the team is a family) understands that training must complement that person's learning style and temperament for a child or athlete to retain what has been taught to him/her. [In the "Coach's Toolbox of Assessments," there is a quick evaluation that coaches can administer to their players, determining the bent of their athletes. It is titled, "Coaching Preference."]

Building Resilience

Resiliency is the ability to bounce back after making a mistake in a game, or when encountering an obstacle, large or small. Elite athletes need to realize that resiliency has to be practiced daily whether they are encountering a major setback like an injury, or something minor like getting cut off in traffic. Author Oliver Poirier-Leroy believes that setbacks and adversity have a way of pushing elite-minded athletes to perform better, not worse. His advice to athletes is to find situations to display resilience: "The problem with wanting to be more resilient is that we only want to be more resilient when things are going our way. When it's easy, when training is going well and there are no bad surprises." He concludes by stating, "It sounds simple, even cliché, but it's true: What doesn't break you, makes you better. It is not that elite athletes don't feel disappointment and frustration that comes when things fall apart; rather it's the way they redirect their anger and focus that makes the difference" (Poirier-Leroy, 2022).

So, how can coaches teach resilience when it seems to be a personal issue athletes must resolve on their own? Here are several suggestions:

First, Coaches can incorporate adverse situations into their practices. When engaged in an intersquad scrimmage, for example, have players "ruff up" the elite players and observe how they react. Then, later in your office, discuss your observations with your athlete and create antidotes for similar treatment during a real game.

Second, after every game, review the game film clips with your athletes, especially how they reacted after an unfair situation or mistake. Seeing oneself on film becomes a powerful learning tool.

Thirdly, many athletes are conditioned to respond to their mistakes in a fatalist manner (called learned helplessness). Bo Hanson, 4x Olympian states that "this condition sees the individual take no action to recover from a failure or unsatisfactory situation because they feel any action will not help them anyway." He went on to say, "Athletes can understand this condition by watching and observing others close to them. This is a negative aspect of the modeling process. It serves as a reminder for coaches that their role is critically important to point out this negative pattern and teach a more positive response" (Hanson, 2022). For example, instead of viewing a particular failure in a negative way, coaches can teach their athletes to view it in a more productive way, choosing to view a mistake as a learning experience for what to do better next time.

And fourthly, according to coach Whitney (Pierce) Miller (1985 Tumbling National Champion, 1986 Tumbling World Age Group Champion, and named Coach of the Year in 2011-12), coaches need to teach their athletes three quotes: *Quote 1*: "If it's easy, it is not worth doing." Coach Miller believes resilience is a byproduct of choosing the harder path. The harder path is most always riddled with challenges, both mentally and physically. Young athletes, according to Coach Miller, can learn a lot from making mistakes. Most coaches see adversity as a negative, but making mistakes is a foundation of all-round growth of an athlete. *Quote 2*: "Contentment is the enemy of ambition; just as good is the enemy of the great." Easy practices are nice, stress free, and comforting, but when you only stay in the comfort zone, ambition and the ability to become resilient is non-existent. It is imperative that the coach give his or her athletes the tools needed to be successful. Gymnastics is 80% mental and 20% physical. The mental aspect of gymnastics, which includes resilience training, is the top priority in training. *Quote 3*: "Emotion has no place in the gym." According to Coach Miller, emotion during training takes away the athlete's mental focus and creates a possible dangerous situation for the athlete. A distracted athlete is an athlete ripe for injury, a major factor that affects resiliency. Feelings, however, are beneficial, normal, and should be embraced, but outside of the gym.

For a player to achieve elite status, coaches need to focus on the multidimensional approach to physical training. Jason Fitzgerald (2012) outlines five types of physical training exercises necessary to prepare elite athletes:

1. Strength exercises, which can be divided into five components: absolute strength (force), general strength (overcoming body weight), power (producing force rapidly), elastic strength (producing force using elastic reflex, like jumping exercises), and strength endurance (sustaining force production).

2. Speed exercises, made up of three sub-categories of acceleration (moving from a stopped position), absolute speed (the highest velocity one can attain), and speed endurance (the ability to maintain absolute speed).

3. Endurance exercises that can be broken down into three sub-qualities of aerobic, fitness, and workload (the ability to withstand a large training load).

4. Flexibility exercises, which include static flexibility (the ability to attain a large range of motion at any joint without any movement—i.e., toe touches), and dynamic flexibility (ability to attain a large range of motion at a joint with accompanying movement—i.e., leg swings).

5. Coordination exercises, which include physical training for agility, mobility, and balance.

Proper physical training increases the odds that elite players will perform better and sustain fewer injuries. As an overseer, coaches need to be abreast of what types and forms of physical training are best for their sport. In addition, they need to encourage their players 1) not to push themselves beyond their body's limits, 2) to perfect their techniques by using good form, 3) to progress slowly, 4) to avoid burnout, and 5) to stay hydrated at all times (Tyndall, 2020).

Coaches of immature athletes, whose bones and muscles are not yet fully developed, must refrain from the temptation to sacrifice their future for the present accolades and benefits of winning today.

Coaching the "Big Three"

Finally, to coach smarter means teaching and often repeating the "Big Three" dimensions of performance success, which are *perception, creativity,* and *intuition.* I dare say, if a poll were taken of coaches, a majority would say that the big three cannot be taught and that players either have or don't have those three abilities built into their DNA. However, research studies have become definitive in the notion that the big three can be taught (Griffin, 2016; Wilson, 2017; Scott, 2004).

Perception: Body Awareness

Perception (or proprioception) is our bodies ability to understand, organize, and interpret sensory information. It allows us to adapt to sudden changes and move quickly and freely without having to consciously think about where we are in our environment. Some have labeled perception as the "6th sense." For example, a person is hiking and sees a large root or rocks on the trail. Based on past learned behavior, the hiker will adjust automatically in such a way as to stabilize the foot and ankle.

Coaches can teach their players to increase their body awareness by conducting various exercises, such as a myriad of balance exercises: dribbling a basketball while wearing glasses with the bottom half of the lenses taped so that the ball cannot be seen, pitching a baseball with eyes closed while visualizing the strike zone, running an obstacle course without looking at the feet, etc.

In summary, greater perceptual training is highly correlated with athletic abilities. Elite athletes demonstrating the greatest levels of perception seem to suffer fewer injuries to the ankles, shoulder, and spine (Han, 2015). Thus, adding body- awareness training to a workout may help athletes perform better and reduce the risk of injury.

Creativity: The Art of Performing the Unknown

How many times have you heard someone say, "I was not born with a creative bent like you are"? That is an incorrect statement, for we all are born with a creative bent. The issue is that we have been programmed to be non-creative by our society. For example, ask a teen standing behind a cash register for change from the ten-dollar bill you gave for an $8.53 purchase. Without the computer in the cash register, some would find it difficult to figure out the change. Our brains have become lazy due to computers doing the work. Another example of the brain going lazy causing loss of creativity is in finding directions from point "A" to point "B." Without the help from the GPS, how many in our culture would be totally lost even with a city map in the car?

Our technological culture has lost the ability to solve problems or find creative ways to retain knowledge because it can be found on our phones. We have become like robots, not having the ability to take creative detours if we are not programmed to do so.

Growing up, I can recall elementary teachers saying, "Now class, how do we color? We color inside the lines." Creativity, by its very nature, encourages us to color outside the lines, exploring possibilities that are not the normal ways of seeing or doing things. Engineer Spencer Silver was commissioned by his company to develop a new stronger adhesive. The product was a failure because the adhesive did not permanently stick to anything, and the company was ready to scrap the project. Spencer, however, did not give up. Five years later, while singing at church, he wondered if he could make a bookmark that would stick to his hymnal but not damage the page after removing it. Immediately his mind went back to the "invention" that didn't work and came up with the idea we now call "Post-it Notes" (Invention of Post-it

Notes, 2022). In this instance, Spencer went outside of the lines to create a new and useful product.

To promote creative elite athletes, coaches need to teach them to think outside of the box, letting them figure out ways to perform that are unique to their temperament, strengths, and weaknesses. Legalistic coaches who deny players the right to play out of the box hinder elite athletes from achieving upper-level skills.

Intuition: Play Without Thinking

Intuition is "(a) quick and ready insight; (b) immediate cognition; (c) knowledge gain by intuition" (Merriam-Webster, 2009). Since most athletic contest decisions must be made in split seconds, the ability to utilize intuition in a sport environment sets elite players apart from good players.

Notice the key words in the definition: "quick," "cognition," "knowledge." Intuition based on a mere "gut" response often leads to disaster (i.e., "ready, shoot, then aim"), yet intuition based on "knowledge" often becomes the very move that wins the game/match. In this instance, the player has transferred validated training options to the subconscious storage bank that can be withdrawn and implemented when a split-second decision is necessary.

Effective coaches believe intuition can be improved with practice by teaching their athletes to consider what may happen before it occurs. Research on intuitive decision-making in sports suggests that effective players develop their instincts through mental rehearsal of potential failures. As cited in Hutson (2019), Gigerenzer's work reveals that athletes who think intuitively can make better split-second decisions because they focus on possibilities rather than rigid rules. By practicing different scenarios mentally, these players build a repertoire of potential solutions they can draw upon in the heat of competition. Rather than being constrained by predetermined responses, they can flexibly adapt to challenges as they arise.

Cross Training and Burnout Prevention

Today, more athletes are specializing in one sport at a younger age and training year-round. In addition, during organized practices or workouts, the same type of drills, conditioning, or repetitive motions are performed over and over. This lack of diversity in both sport and training can lead to overuse injuries or burnout. Increasingly, elite-level athletes are turning to cross-training. Cross training is simply the use of complementary exercises to achieve conditioning goals in order to give primary muscle groups and joints time to rest and recover. It can also help diminish the boredom of doing the same workout routine over and over again.

During the 2021 British Olympic Trials in London, two athletes posted personal bests, including a new world record, arguably as a result of incorporating cross training in their workouts. Stephanie Davis set a new personal record winning the women's marathon while Beth Porter set a new triathlon world record. According to an article published by *Runner's World* (Dennehy, 2021), neither athlete is a high-mileage runner. In fact, of the 25 to 30 hours a week that Potter spent training, only four of those hours were spent running. In addition to cycling and swimming, which are both triathlon disciplines, she also incorporated two strength-training sessions and one yoga session each week (Dennehy, 2021). Davis, a marathon runner, included a "non-impact day" in her weekly training schedule that included swimming in the morning along with the elliptical or riding her trainer in the evening. She would further supplement her running with six to seven hours of cross training each week, including strength and conditioning as well as stretching (Dennehy, 2021).

Martial arts have also become popular as a modality of cross training since it increases an athlete's flexibility, durability, and endurance while developing the entire body's large and small muscle groups (6 Sports, 2023). While the NBA great Shaquille O'Neal has been a longtime fan of mixed martial arts, fellow NBA player Carmello Anthony utilizes boxing in his training:

As athletes, and as basketball players, you have to find different things that can help you on the basketball court. For me, that's boxing. When I'm in the gym, it's me versus you and I don't want to leave that gym with a loss. So that goes into my mindset, and it puts me in that tenacious focus on the basketball court that you just don't want to lose. (6 Sports, 2023, para. 11)

In addition, NFL player Clay Matthews uses mixed martial arts to improve his strength and speed while pro golfer Phil Mickelson has trained in both kung fu and taekwondo to improve conditioning.

Benefits of Cross Training

Too often, the mindset of many highly competitive athletes and coaches is to just work longer and grind harder. This isn't always the best approach. Incorporating cross-training into regular workouts can be very beneficial to elite athletes and help them to achieve better performances. Paul Krause, MD, highlights many of the benefits of cross training:

We've learned over recent years that exercise can both treat and prevent injury and illness. Overdosing on one type of exercise, however, is unhealthy and can result in overtraining injuries, metabolic imbalance, and mental fatigue. In contrast, participating in a variety of exercise activities allows the body to recover from one beneficial stress, while being exposed to another. The symbiotic relationship between these different activities optimizes the training effect on an athlete's physiology. (Krause, 2009, p. 9)

Cross training helps athletes reduce the chance of injury from overuse of muscles and joints while giving connective tissue time to recover and strengthen. It also can help improve overall conditioning, strength, speed, agility, and other specific skills. It can provide flexibility and creativity to routine workouts, keeping the athlete more engaged and less mentally fatigued. It can provide athletes with the opportunity to continue training while injured and can allow athletes of outdoor sports to continue training when weather conditions don't permit outdoor workouts. Athletes can benefit from different types of cross training: weight training, swimming, Pilates, yoga, rowing, martial arts, cycling, jumping rope, elliptical machine, stair climbing, hiking, workout bands, balance training, calisthenics, agility training, or boxing.

Preventing Burnout

One of the most significant advantages of incorporating cross training into a training program is the prevention of burnout. All athletes from time to time get bored or physically or mentally exhausted. Cross training allows for elite-level athletes to stay engaged with workouts and continue skill development and/or conditioning in fresh ways. With the overwhelming amount of time that elite athletes invest in their sport, it's important for all stakeholders including athletes, parents, and coaches, to guard against burnout. Timothy Neal, assistant professor of clinical education at Concordia University in Ann Arbor, Michigan, defined burnout as a combination of physical and emotional exhaustion due to chronic stress of sports or activities without providing proper opportunity to rest and recover (2016). Coaches describe signs and symptoms of burnout to include withdrawal from training, withdrawal from teammates, reduced sense of accomplishment, lack of improvement, and diminished sense of progress (Raedeke et al., 2002).

Most research points to rest and time away from the sport as the best methods to prevent and treat burnout. Cross training can help with this as it provides athletes with the opportunity to continue training while not performing their sport. Having personally spent nearly 30 years in the sport industry, I've witnessed many young athletes deal with burnout, mostly due to overtraining and not allowing their body's time to recover.

Parents can be a big contributing factor in both achieving burnout and preventing burnout in youth. When parents ignore the signs of overtraining and continue to push their child to train or compete, they are involuntarily encouraging burnout. When the young athlete pushes to overtrain, the parent should step in as the adult and provide a mandatory break from training. In a study about coaches' perspectives on athlete burnout published in the *Journal of Sport Behavior* (Raedeke et al., 2002), coaches cited parental pressure as a major cause of burnout. Coaches described some parents who spent a disproportionate amount of time talking with their child on how they were performing in their sport and seemed to be only concerned with the progress the athlete was making (Raedeke et al., 2002). The article cites a particular coach saying that parents who are never satisfied with what their child does cause burnout. The coach mentions how many times athletes achieve personal bests only to hear their parents tell them what they need to do next (Raedeke et al., 2002).

Entrapment can also lead to burnout. Entrapment is when athletes feel as if they are forced to continue participating in a sport even when they may not want to. This can happen due to expectations from parents, coaches, or social groups. It can also occur when the athletes perceive that their identity is tied to their sport; without it, they would feel lost. The athletes may also feel that they have so much time, money, and effort invested in the sport that it would be wrong for them to quit. Life balance is another factor of sport entrapment. Due to training or competition, the young athlete may not be able to participate in social events or other activities and begin to feel resentment towards their sport, eventually leading to burnout.

Overall, it is important for elite level athletes, coaches, and parents to be aware of the signs of burnout and to incorporate prevention strategies, such as rest, cross training, having a healthy personal identity, and better life-balance.

CHAPTER FOUR

The Parent and Physical Cost

Richard Fowler, Stacy Hall, and Holly Haynes

I press on toward the goal to win the prize for which God has called me heavenward in Christ Jesus.
—Philippians 3:14 (NIV)

The Role of the Parent

We parents love our children and are willing to make great sacrifices so that they may experience joy and success. Parenting in general can be difficult as we toggle back and forth between love and discipline, encouragement and accountability, and generosity and financial responsibility. Being a parent of an elite athlete comes with an additional set of expectations and challenges as we may be asked to serve the role of coach, nutritionist, athletic trainer, sports psychologist, fundraiser, and taxi driver. At times, it can be challenging to know exactly what we should be doing and how to do it.

The greatest role we can play is that of the parent and to love unconditionally. No one else can play this role for our son or daughter who happens to be an elite level athlete. Yes, we can provide supporting roles as well, but first and foremost we have to remember that we are their parent first, and the lessons that we teach our children through the parent/child relationship will transcend any success or failure they have during competition.

The first lesson parents can teach their aspiring elite athletes is a *positive worldview* and associated values. As a Christian, I believe that we are all created by God in His own image, and that He loves us for who we are, not whether we win a basketball game or not. God has also blessed us all with individual gifts, talents, and abilities and expects us to utilize those gifts to the fullest. Accordingly, in our home, values such as work ethic, commitment, and integrity take center stage.

We also focus on *perspective*, which is the ability to see the bigger picture in life. Often, it's easy to get lost in the small details of an issue and lose sight of the bigger picture. As an example, my daughter was playing in an elite level junior golf tournament. While playing a par-5, she hit an average tee shot but hit her second shot into the trees, leaving herself with virtually no possibility of hitting the green in regulation. She was very upset and subsequently tried to recover from her misfortune by attempting a highly risky shot which resulted in getting herself into even more trouble and ultimately causing her to double-bogey the hole. This situation gave us the opportunity to have a great discussion about perspective. The tournament was 54 holes. Even though she mishit her second shot, she didn't have to try a highly improbable shot to still be competitive in the tournament. She could have punched out safely, still having an opportunity to get up and down for par, or at worst, possibly bogey. At the time, she was still learning how to be mentally tough on the golf course. When this happened, she became very emotional on the course, believing that she had failed by letting herself down and letting me down and it affected her for several holes. I have found that success in the long run ultimately comes from consistency over a long period–not one instance at bat, one jump shot, one shot on goal, or one stroke. If we teach our kids perspective, it may relieve some of the pressure and allow them to perform better.

Another value that I share with elite athletes is *swagger*. Now, some of you might not consider this a value, but hopefully after reading this section you will agree that it is indeed an important value that parents can help instill in their children. Having spent 27 years of my professional career working in the sports industry, I have had the good fortune to spend some time around Heisman Trophy winners, first-round draft picks, Hall of Fame coaches, and sports industry giants. What they all had in common was swagger. When you read that word, most of you automatically think of bravado, cockiness, or arrogance. That's not at all what I mean, although, yes, some of these athletes were actually very cocky. But the type of swagger I'm talking about is the resolute confidence that exuded from them the moment they stepped on the field of play. This uncanny confidence was rooted in their preparation. They were confident because they knew they worked harder. They were better prepared than their competitors–and they knew it! Swagger is a process. It's real and it's earned.

When parents are able to arm their children with a positive worldview and associated values, it gives the budding athlete the confidence and the ability to deal with all of the many challenges they will face not only in competitive athletics, but also in life.

The Importance of Recovery for the Parent

Parents of active and elite-level athletes can easily get caught in a whirlwind schedule that seems to keep repeating itself–kind of like the movie *Groundhog Day*. We wake up early to make sure our son or daughter gets fed, has their school supplies, and their second bag packed with all of their workout gear. We get them to school, pick them up later and take them to practice or a game which might be over an hour's drive on a weeknight. We rush home to get everyone fed before they start homework and then send them off to bed. On weekends there are tournaments that might require 4:00 AM wake-up calls, terrible hotel breakfasts, and those late-night car rides home. During one memorable golf tournament, the storm was so bad that we went through three umbrellas in one day! We do this because we love our kids and want to help them achieve their goals. What we don't realize is that sometimes all the rushing around, early mornings, late nights, and condensed work schedules, can actually take a toll on our bodies and mental health as well.

Becoming an elite-level athlete and sustaining that level of competition takes a team effort, and a big part of that team is the parent. Just as the athlete must be cognizant of their physical, mental, emotional, and spiritual health, so too must the parent. If you are a planner like me, you may need to schedule a rest day or schedule something fun to do with your family that gives you a break from the mundane day-to-day schedule. Take time to slow down and enjoy some alone time, even if it's just a few hours. Those few solitary hours can do wonders for recharging our souls and helping us to stay sharp. In addition, there may be other important relationships that you have been neglecting that need your attention. I certainly don't do it enough, but I have found when I'm alone and turn off all electronics and just be still, I see things more clearly and gain better perspective. After all, when I'm in a healthier state, I am able to be a better parent, spouse, and friend.

Comparison Traps and the Danger of Overtraining

This second part of this chapter delves into two critical challenges parents face when nurturing their exceptional athletes: the pitfall of comparison and the danger of overtraining. These issues, while seemingly distinct, often intertwine in ways that can significantly impact a young athlete's development and future.

The first section explores the pervasive habit of athlete comparisons. Parents, often unknowingly, fall into the trap of measuring their child against peers or even professional athletes. This constant comparison can lead to unrealistic expectations, potentially undermining the child's confidence and love for the sport. We'll discuss strategies for parents to cultivate a growth mindset in their young athletes, focusing on personal progress rather than external benchmarks.

The second section addresses the crucial issue of overtraining, a concern that cannot be overstated. Despite parents' best intentions to support their child's athletic pursuits, excessive training can lead to burnout, potentially derailing a promising athletic career. We'll examine the physical and psychological impacts of overtraining on young athletes and demonstrate how parents can work collaboratively with their children to establish balanced, effective training regimens.

By understanding and navigating these challenges, parents can play a pivotal role in fostering their children's athletic development while preserving their overall well-being. This chapter aims to equip parents with the knowledge and tools to support their exceptional athletes in a healthy, sustainable manner, ensuring that the joy of the sport remains at the heart of their child's athletic journey.

Comparison Traps

The Role Model Conundrum: Navigating Comparisons in Youth Sports

Parents raising young athletes often encourage their children to observe professional athletes, hoping they will emulate their techniques and work ethic. While this can be beneficial, it presents a significant challenge: allowing children to develop their own athletic identity without falling into the trap of constant comparison.

Avoiding Comparison Traps

As a parent of three athletes who play the same sport, I've experienced firsthand the difficulty of avoiding comparisons. It's a delicate balance to recognize each child's unique abilities and playing style while fostering a supportive family dynamic. This challenge is twofold:

Preventing Internal Family Tensions

When siblings compete in the same sport, it's natural for comparisons to arise. However, these comparisons can lead to resentment, jealousy, and a strained family dynamic. For instance, if one child consistently performs better in games or receives more accolades, the other siblings might feel inadequate or overlooked. Parents must be vigilant in recognizing and celebrating each child's individual strengths and progress, rather than pitting them against each other.

Shielding Children from External Comparisons by Other Parents or Coaches

Beyond the family unit, young athletes often face comparisons from coaches, teammates' parents, and even spectators. These external comparisons can be particularly damaging as they are often based on limited information and can undermine a child's confidence. For example, a well-meaning parent might praise one child's performance while inadvertently criticizing another, saying something like, "Why can't you play as well as Sarah?" Such comments, even if not directed at the child, can create a toxic environment of constant evaluation and judgment.

The Professional Academy Experience

My youngest son's experience in an elite soccer academy illustrates the heightened stakes of comparison. As players approach the age where professional contracts become a possibility, the atmosphere intensifies. Although official depth charts aren't shared, playing time and age group assignments clearly indicate a player's standing.

This system, while designed to motivate players to "fight for the starting spot," can have unintended consequences when parents interfere. Some parents, driven by ambition for their child, may spark unintended rivalries between players. Parents might encourage their children to view teammates as competitors rather than collaborators. This can lead to a breakdown in team cohesion and create a hostile training environment.

Additionally, such behavior can cause frustration and self-doubt in their own children. Constant pressure to outperform others can lead to anxiety and decreased enjoyment of the sport. A child who once loved playing soccer might begin to dread practices and games, viewing them as tests rather than opportunities for growth and fun.

Perhaps most concerning, parents may inadvertently push their children to consider quitting the sport altogether. The weight of expectations and constant comparisons can become overwhelming. Some talented young athletes might choose to walk away from the sport entirely, feeling that they can never measure up to the impossible standards set for them.

The "Notorious Parent" Syndrome

In our academy, there's a parent known for manipulating comparisons to benefit his child. His tactics include comparing other children in specific positions to create openings for his child. This parent might publicly criticize other players' performances or spread rumors about their weaknesses, all in an attempt to make his own child look better by comparison.

Another troubling behavior is encouraging his child to be physically aggressive towards perceived rivals. This behavior not only endangers other players but also teaches his child that unsportsmanlike conduct is acceptable if it leads to personal gain. Additionally, this parent is known for fostering a hostile environment for new trialists (players trying out for the academy). By creating an unwelcoming atmosphere for newcomers, this parent attempts to eliminate potential competition before it even has a chance to establish itself.

This behavior creates a toxic atmosphere and sets a bad example of sportsmanship and ethical conduct for young athletes. It can have long-term negative consequences for both the targeted players and the instigator's own child, who may struggle to form genuine friendships or develop important teamwork skills.

Balancing Competitiveness and Character

While we want to nurture our athletes' competitive spirits, it's crucial to do so without compromising their character or sportsmanship. To achieve this balance, parents should focus on the following skills:

Developing Grit

As defined by psychologist Angela Duckworth, grit is the combination of passion and perseverance for long-term goals. Encourage your child to set personal goals and work consistently towards them, regardless of others' progress. For example, instead of focusing on being the top scorer, a young soccer player might set a goal to improve their weak foot skills over the course of a season.

Fostering a Growth Mindset

Carol Dweck's concept of a growth mindset emphasizes the belief that abilities can be developed through dedication and hard work—praise effort and improvement rather than innate talent or results. For instance, instead of saying, "You're so talented," try "I'm impressed by how hard you've been working on your passing. It's really paying off!"

Encouraging Healthy Role Models

Guide your children towards admiring older, more experienced athletes. This can prevent negative feelings towards peers and promote aspirational thinking. Discuss the journeys of professional athletes, highlighting their struggles and perseverance rather than just their successes.

Praising Specific Achievements

Instead of general praise, focus on particular skills or efforts your child has improved upon. For example, "I noticed you've really improved your corner kicks. Your practice is showing!"

Teaching Emotional Intelligence

Help your child understand and manage their emotions, especially in competitive situations. Discuss how to handle disappointment, frustration, and even success with grace and maturity.

The Power of Words: Parents as Emotional Architects

Children are emotional eavesdroppers, absorbing more from their environment than we often realize. As parents, our words and attitudes shape our children's perceptions of themselves and their sport. To create a positive athletic environment, be mindful of casual comparisons or critiques of other players. Even offhand comments like "Well, at least you're better than Johnny" can foster a harmful comparative mindset. Instead, focus on your child's individual progress and effort.

It's important to focus conversations on personal growth and team dynamics rather than individual rankings. Discuss how your child's skills are improving over time and how they contribute to the team's overall performance. For example, "I loved how you supported your teammates today. Your positive attitude really lifted the team's spirits."

Parents should also discuss the importance of sportsmanship and respect for all players, regardless of skill level. Emphasize that true athleticism includes how one treats others, not just physical prowess. Share stories of professional athletes known for their sportsmanship and character.

Finally, model gracious behavior in both victory and defeat. Your reactions to your child's successes and failures set a powerful example. Demonstrate how to celebrate wins humbly and handle losses with dignity.

Learning Strategies for Supporting Your Elite Athlete

Developing effective communication and support strategies for your young athlete is essential in nurturing both their talent and emotional well-being. The relationship between parent and athlete forms the foundation of their sporting experience, shaping how they perceive challenges, interact with teammates, and ultimately, how they grow within their sport. By thoughtfully approaching how we guide these young athletes, we can help them navigate the complex world of elite sports while maintaining their passion and psychological health. Here are some additional tips to help you effectively support your athlete.

A "Personal Best" Journal

Encourage your child to create a "Personal Best" journal and track their own progress over time, focusing on self-improvement rather than outperforming others. This journal could include specific skills they're working on, personal goals, and reflections on their performances. For instance, a young basketball player might track their free throw percentage over time, setting goals for improvement and reflecting on what techniques work best for them.

A "No Comparison" Rule

Implement a "No Comparison" rule at home. Make it a family policy not to compare siblings or teammates. This doesn't mean ignoring achievements but rather celebrating each child's unique journey. For example, instead of saying, "Why can't you score goals like your sister?" say, "I'm proud of how you're developing your defensive skills. They're crucial for the team's success." A singular focus allows the child to build self-esteem and a positive self-concept.

Perspective-Taking

Teach perspective-taking. Help your child understand that every athlete has their own journey and challenges. Encourage empathy by discussing what other players might be experiencing. For instance, if a teammate is struggling, guide your child in considering what support that teammate might need, rather than seeing it as an opportunity to outshine them.

Diverse Interests

Encourage diverse interests. Support activities outside of their primary sport to develop a well-rounded identity. This not only provides a mental break from the pressures of their main sport but also helps develop different skills and perspectives. For example, a soccer player might benefit from taking up yoga for flexibility and mental focus or joining a debate club to build confidence in communication.

Open Communication

Encourage open communication. Regularly check in with your child about their feelings towards their sport, teammates, and personal progress. Create a safe space where they can express frustrations, doubts, or concerns without fear of judgment. Ask open-ended questions like, "What was the most challenging part of practice today?" or "How do you feel you're progressing towards your goals?"

An Emphasis on the Journey

Emphasize the journey, not just the destination. Help your child understand that becoming a great athlete is a process. Celebrate small victories and learning experiences along the way. For instance, if your child doesn't make the starting lineup, focus on the skills they've improved and how this experience can motivate them to work harder.

Goal-Setting Techniques

Teach goal-setting techniques. Help your child set SMART (Specific, Measurable, Achievable, Relevant, Time-bound) goals. This approach helps shift the focus from comparing themselves to others to achieving personal milestones. For example, instead of "Be the best player on the team," a SMART goal might be "Improve my serve accuracy by 10% over the next three months."

A Team-first Mentality

Encourage a team-first mentality. Help your child understand the value of being a good teammate. Praise actions that contribute to team success, even if they don't show up on the stat sheet. For example, commend them for making a great pass that led to a goal, even if they didn't score it themselves.

A Balanced View of Professional Athletes

Provide context for professional athletes. When discussing pro athletes as role models, provide a balanced view. Share stories of their struggles, setbacks, and the hard work behind their success. This helps children understand that even their heroes faced challenges and weren't always the best.

A Love for the Game

Foster a love for the game. Regularly remind your child why they started playing the sport in the first place. Encourage them to find joy in the process of playing and improving, not just in winning or achieving accolades.

By focusing on personal growth, effort, and character development, parents can help their young athletes navigate the competitive world of sports without falling into the comparison trap. This approach not only fosters a healthier relationship with athletics but also builds resilience and self-awareness that will serve them well beyond their sporting careers. Remember, the goal is not just to raise great athletes, but to nurture well-rounded individuals who can face life's challenges with confidence and grace.

The Danger of Overtraining: A Delicate Balance

As we discussed earlier in this chapter, parents of elite level athletes can serve many different roles in the development of their child but none more important than that of being the parent. As a parent, our first priority must be for the safety and well-being of our child. Now, it may be difficult at times to look at our 6'4", 230-pound son as a child, but no matter how large or old our children become, we parents have an innate ability to see risk before our children do. One such example of risk is overtraining.

Competitive athletes want to compete. They want to out-train their competition so they can win on the field of play. That's a healthy perspective that all elite-level athletes share. But, as we discussed in Chapter 3, there is also a need for rest and recovery to achieve optimal performance. Sometimes, it's difficult for a younger athlete to recognize when their body and/or mind needs a break. They may want to continue their competitive season by playing summer or fall league or try to compete in two leagues at the same time. It's up to parents to be able to read the symptoms associated with overtraining, under-recovery, and burnout and protect their child against it. This may be, at times, an unpopular decision with the child, coach, and peers, but it may be necessary to protect the long-term health, well-being, and competitive success of the young elite athletes. We have listed several symptoms of burnout to consider in Chapter 3.

Some parents, myself included, are very competitive and want to provide every opportunity we can for our kids to be successful. These opportunities might include extended seasons, multiple back-to-back tournaments, dual leagues, etc. But we have to really guard against our own competitive nature and desire to see our kids have short-term success, in order to provide them with the best opportunity to have long-term success and maintain the love of the game.

A big part of this might just be talking with our athletes. I have found that most athletes know when their bodies are screaming for a break but are afraid to say anything to their coach or parent in fear of losing playing time, letting the person down, or facing some other repercussion. I have known several elite-level athletes who played baseball. They played several summer leagues, a fall league, and then played for their high school in the spring–year-round baseball. In a particular instance, an athlete complained extensively about severe soreness, pain, and swelling in their throwing arm, yet his parents continued to urge him to play in tournaments with the hope of securing a college scholarship. This is an example of accepting significant long-term risk for very short-term gain. Missing one tournament in order to recover from severe tendonitis will not stop an elite-level athlete from being recruited. This is a type of situation where parents must step in and put the health and safety of their child first.

Unregulated Overtraining

When training is unregulated, numerous physiological and psychological risks for injury can occur. Unregulated training often holds male and female athletes to the same training standards. In a 2016 study, Sabato et al. found that females competing at the highest level have 20-30% higher incidents of injury than their male counterparts. Unregulated training may cause some athletes to develop eating disorders. This has been a frequent diagnosis for those athletes who participate in gymnastics, wrestling, swimming, and cheerleading.

Unregulated training has been known to cause a myriad of internal maladies. In a 2011 study, Winsley and Matos found that over-trained elite young athletes are more likely to have frequent upper respiratory tract infections, muscle soreness, sleep disturbances, loss of appetite, mood disturbances, shortness of temper, decreased self-confidence, and ability to concentrate if a balanced regimental training is not followed. Unregulated overtraining often leads to negative life stress and poor coping skills (Rogers & Landers, 2005). Unregulated training will alter the body's chemistry, which may result in depression (Frank et al., 2015). Unregulated training may lead the athlete to develop maladaptive perfectionistic tendencies which can result in the athlete sustaining more injuries (Klockare et al., 2022). Unregulated training has caused athletes to develop competition anxiety (Ariza-Vargas 2011).

Regulated Training

During regulated training, strategies should be adopted to ensure positive physical and mental health. Emphasizing neuromuscular development, especially in the lower extremities because 60% of athletic injuries occur in that area (Caine et al., 2006). Being adamant about the use of protective equipment (Russell et al., 2010).

Emphasizing sport rules for safety's sake (Emery, 2010). Including psycho-social factors in training sessions (Main & Grove, 2009). Teaching athletes how to manage stress (Nicolas et al., 2011). Getting positive support from caregivers who show an interest in their young athletes by listening to them and letting them participate in sports decisions (Nicolas et al., 2011).

Even though parents delegate coaching responsibilities to the coach, they still play a crucial role in overseeing the physical and psychological development of their child as if they were an "athletic director." Both parents and student-athletes should understand the importance of structured training that promotes a balanced life, including relationships, academics, spirituality, recreation, and sports participation. It's wise for parents to remind themselves and their children that sports should be about play, enjoyment, and physical activity for personal pleasure, not just about winning.

To maintain this perspective, thoughtful parents might consider a daily reminder of sport's true essence. Wise parents may want to place a sign on the bathroom mirror that reads, "Sport is play, frolic, and fun; a source of diversion with physical activity for personal pleasure." Winning will be the result, not the aim! Parents should prioritize enjoyment, personal growth, and holistic development over an obsessive focus on victory.

CHAPTER FIVE

The Athlete and Mental Cost

Richard Fowler and Holly Haynes

Can't nobody stop me, yeah, they clockin' in on a stormy day
Okay, line 'em up
Covers off, everything I gotta give I'ma give away
Okay, line 'em up
My body told me it can't really see me on
Nothing better than a bed I'm sleepin' on
But I'ma keep grinding 'til it rain
Then when I bounce back I get a raise
They tried to tell us to hold the line
But I've been over that, I'm helpin' overtime
I know you noticed it ain't no decline
It's so wild, but I tone it down
Ayy, can't invest, yeah, my brain a mess
Ayy, Lord knows every day I rest
Uh, even then I gotta strive
To keep the end goal in my eyes...
—Trip Lee, "No Days Off"

Everyone says that the most important key to an athlete's success is their mindset. That may well be true. In fact, mindset is critical to overall success. Many think it is just a positive mindset that is necessary. However, success for athletes will require a mental cost. It is a combination of mindset, grit, and taking care of one's mental health.

My daughter tore two major ligaments in her knee prior to her college career. The first time, she tore her meniscus. It was an overuse injury, and she was coming off her best year of pre-collegiate play. Since she was in the middle of college recruitment, she was passionate about returning to the field. However, in the middle of her training, her physiologist, Chad Cook, mentioned that successful return to play was not just about physical rehabilitation. She also needed to work on her mindset. You see, injury is trauma. Her brain was going to try to prevent her from experiencing pain again. So, the fear when she moved her knee a certain way would trigger the brain and possibly shut down her desire to move in that direction. So, she took it to heart and worked on training her body to be comfortable with every direction of movement. However, as she did that with her body, she used her determination to propel herself back to the field. She used a combination of mindset and grit to ground herself positively. She had the support of parents, coaches, and grandparents, which greatly helped her mental health and allowed her to dispel fear of re-injury and fear of contact in a contact sport.

My daughter's story following her first injury was a positive one, but that is not the case for many athletes. And her second injury proved to be one that would test her mental health, tenacity, and mindset. While the first injury took 9 months to get back to full-field play, the second injury was only supposed to take 6 months to return to play. She returned to the field in 6 months, but she missed her first season of collegiate play. She had always been a starter. Even though her first injury required surgery, and this one did not, the circumstances around recovery were a little different, and the stakes were a little higher. When she was injured previously, she had the support of family and coaches. She was team captain—had been for two years. She knew no one could match what she brought to her team. The second time around, she was an unknown—the newbie. No one knew what she brought to the team. This time, fear crept into her recovery process. Would she be good enough to earn some playing time? Could she be good enough now that she had to play with a brace? How would she have to adjust? While she asked these questions following her injury, many athletes struggle with similar concerns throughout their careers: *Am I good enough? Am I fast enough? Am I strong enough?*

So, what is the answer to questions of doubt and fear that can cloud an athlete's mind? Mindset, grit, and good mental health.

Mindset

Mindset as we will use it for the purpose of this book was defined by Carol Dweck (2016). Dweck posits that there are two types of mindsets that people possess: fixed or growth. Ideally, all people, including successful athletes, should possess a *growth* mindset. But what is a *growth* mindset? Well, it is one that understands that effort is more important than given ability. Many athletic motivational speakers talk about this idea of "grindin," or "no days off," effort. However, while that individual drive to work hard is a given for many athletes, doubt can creep into the young athletes as they are developing. So, while they may be working hard on their craft, if they see others receiving more praise or receiving more awards or even playing time, athletes may begin to doubt their ability. If we tell ourselves, "I'm just not as smart as that person," that can be detrimental when it shuts down our effort. You see, we all assess ourselves in relation to others. However, if we assess ourselves to be less than and have a *fixed* mindset, we settle for just being less than. If we assess ourselves to be less than and develop a drive or passion to work harder, then we have a *growth* mindset. Growth mindset places the effort on deliberate practice, not solely on ability. According to Dweck, "Becoming is better than being." She further states, "No matter what your ability is, effort is what ignites that ability and turns it into accomplishment." So, the pursuit is just as important as the product. Growth mindset affords an athlete the ability to keep pushing despite obstacles thrown in their path (e.g., injury).

Sometimes the biggest obstacle for athletes can be their parents. Yes, winning is important. However, the successful athlete is not just concerned about winning or losing. They are concerned about how they play. Dweck says this of parents:

> Parents think they can hand children permanent confidence—like a gift—by praising their brains and talent. It doesn't work, and in fact has the opposite effect. It makes children doubt themselves as soon as anything is hard or anything goes wrong. If parents want to give their children a gift, the best thing they can do is to teach their children to **love challenges**, **be intrigued by mistakes**, **enjoy effort**, and **keep on learning**. That way, their children don't have to be slaves of praise. They will have a lifelong way to build and repair their own confidence (Dweck, 2006, p. 17).

Dweck's insights reveal how well-intentioned praise can actually undermine an athlete's development. When parents focus solely on talent or results, they inadvertently create fragile confidence that crumbles in the face of adversity. Instead, by celebrating effort, resilience, and the learning process itself, parents can help build lasting self-assurance that withstands challenges.

This understanding of mindset and motivation leads us to examine another crucial aspect of athletic development: the cost of buying mental toughness. While proper praise and encouragement lay the foundation, athletes must also develop specific mental skills to achieve elite status.

The Cost of Mental Toughness

All athletes who have set the goal to be elite must buy into a mindset which is becoming rarer and rarer in Western society—*mental toughness*. Part of that mindset is the commitment to learn a sport, practice that sport, and submit to the rigors and conditioning of that sport. However, agreeing to buy into the mental toughness component, which engenders elitism, may be the most expensive purchase an athlete makes. Many athletes with great talent lose out because they have failed to realize that mental toughness is the hub on the wheel of success. All other athletic components are but spokes which that hub supports.

Dr. Patrick J. Cohn, a leader in sport psychology, defines mental toughness in this way:

- Mental toughness is being a competitor in all situations.
- Mental toughness is continuing to fight to play your best the last few games of the season when your team has already been eliminated from the playoffs.
- Mental toughness is pushing yourself to the limit during the last five minutes of practice.

During a workshop with athletes, he went on to say, "The reality is that every time you compete, you succeed. You may not succeed in winning the contest, but you succeed in building your mental toughness, because every time you compete, you invest in your mental toughness" (Cohn, 2018).

For athletes to reach their full potential, then, mental toughness needs to be developed and refined on a regular basis. So, how do they do that? Let's consider several factors:

Factor 1: Mindfulness

In recent years, the term *mindfulness* has bombarded the psychological/counseling world and is now widely used in most therapeutic settings. However, the word has been around for many decades. On many occasions, for example, my mother would say things like, "Now, before you do x or y, I want you to be *mindful* of the consequences of your decision." What did she mean by that, and how does that kind of mindfulness affect an athlete's mental toughness?

Mindfulness can be defined as a way of paying deliberate and concentrated attention to the "here and now" (what's going on presently in our mind, body, and environment), and possessing the ability to quickly sort through those findings in order to find solutions that will not hinder forward progress. Mindfulness gives athletes the ability to overcome mental obstacles by paying close attention to thoughts and feelings that occur when playing sports (Kaufman et al., 2018).

The Mind

Mentally tough elite athletes have learned to harness a negative thought ("I did not perform well; therefore, I must not be as good as I thought") and turn it into the positive ("I had a poor performance, yet after evaluation, I realized I was playing cards until 3 am, and did not get eight hours of sleep prior to the game. And so, to correct this, I will choose and determine not to allow that behavior again").

The Body

Mentally tough athletes have learned "to listen to their body" (a discussion which was addressed in chapter 3). Active listening is not only being cognizant of what is going on in one's body and keeping a frontal cortex awareness of bodily sensation, but also adjusting responses accordingly. For example, being conscious of how one is breathing can prevent fatigue from occurring in a game or contest. Understanding that anxiety and frustration speed up metabolism, an elite athlete can learn to calm the sympathetic nervous system (fight, flight, or freeze syndrome) resulting in increased performance.

The Environment

Mentally tough athletes have learned to control how they react to the environment. For example, in a game situation where there are many rowdy hecklers, elite athletes have already anticipated fan chaos in that environment and have programed their minds to tune out distractions around the field or court which may trigger unhelpful emotions.

Factor 2: Visualization

Mental toughness is enhanced when elite athletes can *visualize* personal success and continue to picture that success even when a game or contest is not going their way (Blankert, 2017). For example, a basketball player who has missed four three-point shots in a row is still convinced, in a proactive way, that the next three-point shot will go in, making the odds of that happening go up significantly.

According to Hannah Elizabeth Jones, M.D. (three-time national gymnastic and tumbling athlete, 2010-2012), the practice of visualization was the key factor in her athletic success. Dr.

Jones stated, "Visualization was one of the most impactful parts of practice. This meant closing our eyes and running through each routine perfectly over and over. This practice allowed us to see ourselves doing our skills perfectly during competition before we ever got there. So, when the big day came, it felt as if we had already done this a million times before and made us feel more in control."

So, how can visualization be learned? It can be learned by implementing the "Visualization Exercise for Athletes."

Step 1

Athletes are asked to write down and describe a situation(s) where they (a) achieved the best athletic performance of their life; (b) felt the most connected to their teammates; and (c) remember a season when their attitude was at its very best, putting out 100% and feeling good and energized for doing it. Once they have completed this written assignment, they go to the next step.

Step 2

For the next six days, athletes are encouraged to find a secluded place where they can spend five minutes a day visualizing what was written down in those three areas. They are asked to focus on one domain per day, cycling through each of the domains throughout the six days. When focusing on one of the three domains, they are asked to imagine the sights, sounds, and feelings that surrounded the events they experienced. They are reminded that it is common to feel distracted during this visualization exercise. If this happens, athletes simply return their thoughts to the exercise once they become aware of the drifting and start the five-minute exercise over again.

Step 3

Prior to an athletic contest, athletes are encouraged to revisit the three areas again and transfer those feelings to the upcoming game/meet/match situation and continue to see those images on the "TV" in their brain for the entire event. That is how a player who has missed four three-point shots can continue to see "nothing but net" on the fifth three-point attempt.

Step 4

The final step in the visualization exercise is the "player performance personal feedback analysis." In this self-analysis, athletes are requested to answer five questions in writing:

1.   On a scale of 1-10 (10=awesome), how would I rate myself on the performance goals I set for myself for the game just played?

2.   What are some specific incidents where I missed the mark regarding the performance goals I set for myself?

3.   How would I rate my mental attitude (scale 1-10; 10=awesome) during the game just played? If not a 9 or 10, why?

4.   In the game just played, how would I rate my role as a team player (scale 1-10)? If not a 9 or 10, why?

5.   Based on the above data, what are my improvement goals for the upcoming week?

Consistently following this formula will increase player confidence and mental toughness.

Factor 3: Astute Student of The Game

Mentally tough athletes are keenly astute observers and diligent learners of the game. They can accurately assess situations or people and turn them to their own advantage. Furthermore, these elite athletes understand their imperfections, desire to be coached, and are humble in spirit. In summary, the astute student of the game can be described as *coachable*.

So, what are the characteristics of a *coachable* athlete? Lindsey Wilson, co-founder of Positive Performance Mental Training Zone lists ways elite athletes obtain mental toughness through being coachable (Wilson, 2022). Five on her list include:

1.   Coachable athletes are not caught up in their own notoriety. They listen to what their coaches say.

2.   Coachable athletes understand that their coaches really want the best for their players and trust them.

3.   Coachable players act like adults and will look their coaches in the eye. Rolling eyes as a sign of displeasure

is immature and is not characteristic of the mentally tough athlete.

4. Coachable players are in constant communication with the coach and do not "stuff" resentment, or harbor negative thoughts about the team or coach. Instead, coachable athletes are desirous of team unity and will engage in active discussions with their coaches, seeking possible positive solutions to game strategy differences.

5. Coachable players are known for their gratitude.

The coach-player dynamic is only one of the multitude of aspects and possibilities that elite athletes face. But it is hugely important because receiving criticism in any area of life is tough. However, being able to graciously receive advice and mentorship is a large part of growing mentally tough.

Factor 4: Embracing the True Definition of Success

Finally, to be genuinely mentally tough is to *embrace the true definition of success*, which is to keep sports in proper perspective. Years ago, Tom Osborne, former head coach at the University of Nebraska, summarized his view of success after competing in the Orange Bowl for the national championship. Reflecting on his career and his team's successes, Osborne wrote,

> I sat in my hotel room after the game reflecting on what had just transpired and realized that it really isn't so much about achieving the end result—the national championship and the trophies, which are all fine. But the important thing about athletics really is the process. It is the path you follow in attempting to win the important championship. The relationships formed, the effort given, and the experiences you have. And when it is all over, it's over. Everything else, at least for me, was anti-climax.

> Athletics is a hard taskmaster; some of the key factors such as PATs, officiating, and injuries aren't really in our hands. The most critical thing, however, isn't the adversity. It is how we react to adversity. I see a lot of pain in athletics. The saving grace of it all, as far as I'm concerned, is the

knowledge that out of pain and adversity so often we develop mental toughness, and our character becomes evident.

I've gotten away from measuring success in terms of wins and losses. I measure success more in terms of how close a team has come to realizing its potential (1985, p. 124, 144).

So, what is true success? It is a process. It does not hinge on external sources but is based on inward satisfaction. It is reaching one's potential. It takes a mentally tough athlete to come to those conclusions.

Portrait of a Mentally Tough Elite Athlete

At the outset, we stated that for elite athletes to reach their full potential, they must buy into the mental toughness component. Mentally tough athletes develop healthy habits, some of which are observable:

1. Being open to taking calculated risks.
2. Letting go of what they can't control.
3. Learning from past mistakes and moving on.
4. Being flexible and open to change.
5. Cherishing alone time to meditate on their game.
6. Not blaming the environment or others for having a bad game.
7. Taking responsibility for their decisions.
8. Never giving up.
9. Managing their emotions.
10. Realizing they can't please everyone.
11. Not engaging in "pity" parties.
12. Working overtime to perfect their game.
13. Always looking for ways to improve.
14. Not being jealous of teammate successes.
15. Being able to focus on the big picture.

A challenge for all athletes is to evaluate each of the above factors and beside each, rank, on a scale of 1-10 (10=100% accurate of me), how they fare. If the score is eight or below, what strategies can be put in place to bring that toughness score to a 9 or 10?

CHAPTER SIX

The Coach and the Mental Game

Richard Fowler and Stacy Hall

*"Not many of you should become teachers, my fellow believers, because you know
that we who teach will be judged more strictly."*
—James 3:1 (NIV)

Coaches: Superheroes in Disguise?

Ever watched a coach in action and thought, "Wow, they must have superpowers!"? Well, you're not far off. On any given day, coaches juggle a mind-boggling array of tasks: recruiting new talent, chatting with parents and administrators, creating practice plans, managing equipment, fundraising, and even playing psychologist, nutritionist, and motivator—all rolled into one! It's like they're wearing a dozen different hats at once.

But here's the kicker—coaches aren't actually superheroes. They're very much human, dealing with the same stressors we all face. The difference? They're doing it under the spotlight, with the pressure of wins and losses and the future of young athletes resting on their shoulders. It's a unique challenge that requires a special kind of resilience.

Beyond the X's and O's

Thousands of books have been written about coaching, mostly focusing on mastering the game–you know, the X's and O's of winning strategies. But the truly great coaches? They've got something extra up their sleeves. They're not just tactical geniuses; they're also top-notch psychologists who know how to bring out the best in their players. Think about the coaches who've made history–they didn't just know the game inside and out, they knew people. They could read a player's body language, understand what motivates each individual, and create an environment where everyone felt challenged yet supported. That's a skill that goes way beyond any playbook.

And here's another secret ingredient: they've mastered the art of managing their own mental and emotional fatigue. It's this skill that allows them to perform at an elite level, inspiring their team to do the same. After all, how can you lead others if you're running on empty yourself?

In this chapter, we're diving into the mental cost of coaching elite athletes (Don't worry, we'll tackle the emotional side later in the book!). These two aspects are crucial to coaching, but they're different beasts. *Mental exhaustion* is all about those cognitive skills–thinking, memory, decision-making, and problem-solving. It's what happens when your brain feels like it's been put through a wringer after a tough game. *Emotional exhaustion*, on the other hand, deals with feelings–identifying, processing, and expressing them (Santos-Longhurst & Raypole, 2022). That's more about the heart than the head, if you will.

When we talk about exhaustion, we're basically talking about fatigue. A study by Russell et al. (2019) defines mental fatigue as "a psychobiological state caused by prolonged periods of demanding cognitive activity shown to negatively influence physical performance." In other words, it's what happens when your brain has been working overtime without a break. Sound familiar, coaches? It's like trying to run a marathon after pulling an all-nighter–not exactly a recipe for peak performance.

Spotting the Signs of Mental Fatigue

Let's face it—coaches are in it to win it. They want everyone, including themselves, to perform at their absolute best. But this drive for excellence can put both athletes and coaches under immense daily stress. It's like being on a high-wire act, day in and day out, with no net below. Those who consistently perform at an elite level are usually better equipped to handle these pressures. They've developed mental calluses, so to speak. However, it's crucial to recognize when stress is starting to take a toll on performance.

Just like we've discussed in earlier chapters about under-recovery, overtraining, and burnout, mental fatigue can be prevented if you catch it early. It's like noticing a small leak in a boat–fix it early, and you're smooth sailing. Ignore it, and well, you might find yourself sinking fast.

So, what should you be on the lookout for? Santos-Longhurst and Raypole (2022) suggest that mental fatigue can creep in when your brain is bombarded with too many stimuli or has to maintain intense activity without rest. Does this sound like a typical day in coaching? Thought so! It's like your brain is a smartphone that's constantly running all its apps at once–eventually, that battery is going to drain. Here are some behaviors that might signal mental fatigue in coaches:

- Disengagement (Coach seems less invested than usual)
- Decreased motivation and enthusiasm (Where's that usual fire?)
- Increased emotional outbursts (Short fuse, anyone?)
- Tendency to withdraw (Suddenly less communicative)
- Changes in concentration (Trouble focusing during practice)
- Decreased discipline (Letting things slide that usually wouldn't)
- Decreased attention to detail (Missing the little things)
- Feeling like your brain is 'too full' (Information overload!)

When coaches experience these symptoms, they're not at their best, and that can impact the whole team. It's like a domino effect: when the coach is off their game, it ripples through the entire squad.

Here's an important truth I've observed in my 27 years in sports: coaches are tough, confident, competitive individuals who usually focus on everyone else. They're the captains of the ship, always looking out for their crew. But to reach their peak performance, they need to tune into their own physical, mental, and emotional well-being too. It's the classic airplane oxygen mask scenario–you've got to take care of yourself before you can effectively help others.

Winning Strategies for Managing Mental Fatigue

Good news! Once you spot the signs of mental fatigue, there are plenty of strategies to tackle it head-on. Even better, most of these tactics can help prevent mental fatigue in the first place. Think of it as a playbook for your brain. Let's break them down:

Embrace Your ZZZs

Coaches often burn the midnight oil, reviewing game tapes or perfecting strategies. But skimping on sleep isn't sustainable. It's like trying to drive a car without refueling–eventually, you're going to sputter to a stop. Aim for that full 7-8 hours–your brain (and your team) will thank you!

Find Mini Mental Vacations

Take brief breaks from the constant stimulation. Turn off the electronics, step away from the noise, and give your brain a breather. A short walk or even a power nap can work wonders. It's like hitting the reset button on your mental computer. Fun fact: Florida State University's legendary football coach Bobby Bowden was known for his pre-practice naps! If it's good enough for a coaching legend, it's good enough for the rest of us.

Schedule Downtime

Just like you plan practice sessions, plan time to completely shut off. Quality beats quantity here. Maybe pick up a hobby or do something you enjoy away from coaching duties. It could be fishing, woodworking, reading, or even learning a new skill unrelated to sports. This isn't just leisure time; it's maintenance for your mental machinery.

Get Moving

Exercise isn't just for athletes! It's a great stress reliever that can improve sleep, nutrition choices, mood, and mental sharpness. Win-win-win-win! Plus, it sets a great example for your team. You're practicing what you preach about the importance of physical activity.

Set Realistic Goals

Coaches, be sure to set realistic goals. Pushing limits is important, but consistently setting unreachable goals adds unnecessary stress. Balance ambition with realism to avoid mental fatigue. It's okay to shoot for the stars, but make sure you've got a solid rocket ship first.

Prioritize Like a Pro

Time is a coach's most precious resource, so prioritize like a pro. Focus on tasks that truly move your program forward. Ask yourself: Is this helping my team? Can it be done more efficiently? Can someone else handle it? Don't be afraid to delegate or even drop tasks that don't make the cut. Remember, busy doesn't always mean productive.

Cover the Basics

Coaches, be sure to cover the basics. Santos-Longhurst and Raypole (2022) remind us not to neglect our fundamental needs:

- Nutrition: Aim for a balanced diet and stay hydrated. Your brain needs fuel just like your body does.
- Physical Activity: Even if a full workout isn't possible, try yoga, gardening, or a neighborhood stroll. Every bit of movement counts.

- Sunlight and fresh air: Spend some time outdoors each day. Nature has a way of clearing the mental cobwebs.

- Social Support: Share your experiences with loved ones – it's not just about emotional support but sometimes getting tangible help too. Remember, even coaches need coaching sometimes.

Implementing these strategies isn't just about avoiding burn-out; it's about optimizing your performance as a coach. When you're mentally fresh, you're more creative in your strategies, more patient with your athletes, and more resilient in the face of challenges. It's an investment in yourself that pays dividends for your entire team.

Remember, a mentally fresh coach leads to a stronger team. By taking care of their own mental game, coaches set themselves–and their athletes–up for success. It's not selfish; it's necessary. You wouldn't expect your car to run without regular maintenance, so why expect that from your brain?

Parents and athletes, you play a role too! Recognizing the demands on coaches and offering support can make a big difference. Maybe it's volunteering to help with some tasks, being understanding when the coach needs a moment to recharge or simply expressing appreciation for their hard work. After all, sports are a team effort, both on and off the field.

So, next time you see your coach looking a bit frazzled, remember–they're running their mental marathon. A little understanding and support can go a long way in helping them cross that finish line strong! And coaches, don't be afraid to prioritize your mental well-being. Your team needs you at your best, and that starts with taking care of yourself.

In the end, managing mental fatigue isn't just about avoiding the negative; it's about unlocking your full potential as a coach. When you're mentally sharp, you're not just surviving the season–you're thriving, innovating, and inspiring. And isn't that what great coaching is all about?

CHAPTER SEVEN

The Mental Role of Parents

Holly Haynes

> *"For one so small, you seem so strong*
> *My arms will hold you, keep you safe and warm*
> *This bond between us can't be broken*
> *I will be here, don't you cry"*
> —Phil Collins, "You'll Be in My Heart"

Parenting an elite athlete is a journey filled with unique challenges and rewards. As we've explored in previous chapters, there are numerous elements parents must juggle to help their young athletes strive for excellence while remaining grounded and humble. This delicate balance requires parents to be not just supporters, but also emotional anchors, logistical coordinators, and wise guides through the complex world of elite sports.

The demands on parents of elite athletes are significant. Beyond the physical support of driving to practices, games, and tournaments, there's an enormous emotional component. Parents must remain level-headed under pressure, provide unwavering emotional support, and maintain a structured environment conducive to their child's growth. This can be especially taxing after long weeks filled with regular practices, competitions, and private lessons.

In this high-pressure environment, it's crucial for parents to maintain their own sense of self. Becoming too engrossed in their child's athletic pursuits can lead to a loss of personal identity, potentially diminishing their ability to provide effective support. Therefore, striking a balance between focusing on your child's goals and maintaining stability in your own life is paramount for both your well-being and that of your young athlete.

The Mental Health Imperative

In today's athletic landscape, addressing mental health and building mental fortitude is more critical than ever. The case of Simone Biles, the Olympic champion gymnast, provides a powerful illustration of this point. Biles faced significant criticism when she withdrew from several events during the 2021 Tokyo Olympics, citing mental health concerns. This decision, however, sparked a crucial conversation about the mental toll of elite sports.

Shortly after the Olympics, the world learned of the trauma many top gymnasts had endured at the hands of their team doctor. This revelation underscored that trauma can surface at any time, even under the intense pressure of Olympic competition. It's a stark reminder that athletes, despite their superhuman abilities, are fundamentally human. They are subject to the same stressors and emotional responses as anyone else, including the activation of the fight-or-flight response under extreme pressure.

As parents, it's our responsibility to equip our young elite athletes with strategies to cope with these challenges. However, it's equally important that we model these practices ourselves. Our children learn as much from our actions as from our words.

Parents as the "Home Coach"

Establishing yourself as the "home coach" is a vital yet challenging role for parents of elite athletes. This position goes beyond cheering from the sidelines; it involves being a constant source of emotional support, guidance, and structure.

Dr. Lisa Damour, a renowned clinical psychologist, emphasizes the critical role parents play in shaping their children's emotional development (2024). While modern parenting faces unique challenges, such as social media pressures and societal tensions, the fundamental need for parental guidance remains unchanged. She points out that parents must be especially attuned to their children's emotional needs in sports, where performance pressure and peer comparison can create additional stress. Studies have shown that children whose parents provide consistent emotional support and validation are better equipped to handle the mental rigors of athletic competition (Kramers et al., 2023).

Drawing from Diana Baumrind's research, we know that an authoritative parenting style—which balances high expectations with high responsiveness and warmth—tends to lead to better outcomes than either overly strict (authoritarian) or overly permissive approaches (1971). This style provides children with the boundaries, guidance, and emotional support they need to thrive. Research consistently shows that children of authoritative parents develop stronger self-regulation skills and emotional resilience. These qualities prove especially valuable in athletic settings, where young athletes must navigate both success and disappointment.

As parents, we can be our children's biggest cheerleaders while providing constructive support. This involves being attuned to our children's emotional development within their sport. Dr. Damour (2024) notes a concerning trend where difficult emotions are often dismissed or mishandled. For instance, if a child expresses sadness over a string of losses and withdraws to their room, parents might hastily interpret this as depression rather than taking the time to discuss and process these feelings with their child. Young athletes need space to experience and work through their emotions in a supportive environment.

It is crucial for parents to create an environment where children feel safe expressing all emotions, not just positive ones. By establishing ourselves as trustworthy confidants, we enable our children to share their struggles openly. This foundation of trust becomes especially important during challenging moments in sports, where emotions can run exceptionally high. Creating this safe space requires consistent, empathetic responses even to difficult emotions like anger, fear, or disappointment.

The way parents handle these emotional moments can have lasting impacts on both athletic development and personal growth. When children feel emotionally supported, they are more likely to take healthy risks and persist through challenges. Understanding how to navigate these situations effectively often comes through real-world experience. Learning from others' experiences can provide valuable insights into managing similar situations with our own young athletes.

A Personal Anecdote: Navigating Emotional Challenges

Consider this recent example: A friend's son faced a distressing situation during a game where he was subjected to derogatory name-calling. Although the club swiftly addressed the issue, the child was overwhelmed with emotion. After the game, safe in their car, he broke down in tears.

This moment called for careful parental response. It wasn't a time for phrases like "boys don't cry" but rather an opportunity for emotional support. The parents listened as their son cried and questioned the other child's actions. Their established trust allowed the child to be vulnerable with them. Only after this emotional release did they discuss strategies for handling future verbal assaults.

This scenario underscores the importance of creating a safe space for children to express their emotions. It also highlights the long-term nature of an elite athlete's journey, which is filled with both triumphs and challenges. As parents, we spend more time with our young athletes than their coaches do, giving us a unique opportunity to build a strong emotional foundation.

Maintaining Mental Calm Under Pressure

One of the most crucial skills for parents of elite athletes is maintaining composure when their child is under pressure. This requires emotional maturity and the ability to separate yourself from your child's performance. Here are key strategies:

1. Recognize signs of stress in your child: These can include physical symptoms like changes in appetite or sleep patterns, emotional signs such as irritability or withdrawal, or behavioral changes like perfectionism or avoidance.

2. Develop personal calming techniques: Practice mindfulness, meditation, or controlled breathing exercises. These can help you remain calm in high-stress situations.

3. Model composure: Your child will learn from your behavior. Demonstrate how to handle pressure and setbacks with grace.

4. Separate your emotions from your child's performance: Remember, your child's athletic journey is their own. Avoid living vicariously through their achievements or failures.

Communication is key in this process. Regular, open conversations with your child about their feelings and experiences can help you understand their emotional state and provide appropriate support. These discussions should happen not just after difficult moments, but also during times of success and routine practice, establishing a pattern of open dialogue that makes it easier for children to come forward during challenging times. Creating these consistent channels of communication helps parents recognize subtle changes in their child's emotional well-being and address potential issues before they become overwhelming.

A Personal Example: The Taekwondo Test

Let me share a personal experience that illustrates the importance of recognizing and addressing your child's stress. When our daughter was about 7, she was progressing well in her taekwondo classes. She enjoyed attending and was moving through her belts at a solid pace. However, as she approached her yellow belt test, something changed.

One of the test requirements was to memorize a Bible verse, which was longer than usual for this level. Our daughter, typically a quick study, hadn't prepared adequately. As we pulled into the parking lot for her test, she suddenly asked if she could quit the taekwondo classes. Her beautiful, large eyes welled up with tears, and she pleaded with me not to force her to go inside.

This moment called for careful listening and support. It was not about her ability to break a board or perform the physical aspects of the test. When I asked if she had memorized the Bible verse, she admitted she had not and was afraid of failing the test. This was my firstborn perfectionist child, not wanting to face the possibility of failure.

We used this as a teachable moment. We discussed the importance of preparation and how this situation could have been avoided. We practiced the Bible verse in the car, and she went on to pass her test. This experience became a stepping stone, and she later won several competitions and earned two black belts.

This example shows how important it is to listen closely to your child and help them choose the best option for them—not for you. It also demonstrates how a little listening and support can go a long way in helping children overcome their fears and achieve their goals.

The Impact of Parental Pressure

Another crucial aspect of maintaining mental calm is understanding the impact of parental pressure on your child and their teammates. I remember a telling incident with my son's team. He once said about a teammate: "If he doesn't play aggressively, his mom is gonna beat him." This comment reveals the intense pressure some children face from their parents. Not only was that child under stress, but his teammates were aware of it too. The child had become an extension of the parent, with no separation between the parent's ambitions and the child's performance.

In this case, the parent lived vicariously through the child. There was no time for normal childhood activities like sleepovers—just continual training and focus on the game. The child struggled with emotional composure, particularly with aggressive emotions, as this was the behavior rewarded by the parent.

This example serves as a cautionary tale. As parents, we need to ensure we are not setting unrealistic expectations for our children. Instead, we should focus on supporting their dreams and goals in a healthy, balanced way.

Values-Based Parenting in Elite Sports

An often overlooked aspect of raising elite athletes is values-based parenting. As your child progresses in their sport, they will face numerous challenges, many of which you won't be present to help navigate. By instilling strong values, you provide them with an internal compass to guide their decisions and actions.

Consider what virtues you want your child to embody. Do you prioritize integrity, sportsmanship, perseverance, or humility? Remember, the goal isn't just to raise a great athlete but to nurture a well-rounded individual who contributes positively to society.

For example, if your child refuses to shake hands with a coach after being substituted early, use this as a teachable moment about respect and sportsmanship. These lessons extend far beyond the playing field and shape your child's character for life.

F. Stuart Sanders, M.D. (Olympic and U. S. Figure Skating Team physician, internal and sport medicine specialist, and adjunct professor of cardiology at Emory University School of Medicine), when asked in an interview what values parents should inculcate into the minds of their elite athletes, suggested the following (personal communication, November 22, 2023):

1. Have your children participate in several sports to enhance their athlete skills.
2. Teach your children to have fun and enjoy the sport they are involved in.
3. Emphasize academics.
4. Insist that your elite athlete practice good sportsmanship. Compete to win fairly but realize that there is no dishonor in losing. This applies to sports and to the

challenges of life. As the Olympic creed says, "All honor to those who fall and rise again."

5. Never allow your children to use performance-enhancing substances to achieve a "win at all costs" goal.

6. Make sure your elite athletes stay well rounded, enjoying life outside of sports.

7. In winning or losing, always be gracious. Thank God, your family, your friends and coaches that have enabled you to compete.

8. Elite athletes can sometimes become self-absorbed, so parents make time to care for and share with those who are perhaps less talented and less fortunate.

9. As parents, check yourselves to make sure you are not living your dreams through your elite athlete.

10. And finally, love your children because they are your children, not because they are promising athletes. As I Timothy 4:8 says, "For physical training (or athletic accolades) is of some value, but godliness is profitable for all things."

These values reflect a holistic approach to athletic development that prioritizes character formation alongside physical achievement. Each point emphasizes the importance of maintaining perspective and balance, recognizing that sports are a means of personal growth rather than an end in themselves. Dr. Sanders' guidelines particularly underscore the need for parents to view their children as whole people, not just athletes. His emphasis on gratitude, humility, and spiritual development provides a framework for raising well-adjusted individuals who can succeed both in sports and in life.

The transition from youth sports to elite athletics can often blur these fundamental values. Parents may feel increasing pressure to focus solely on athletic achievement as the stakes get higher and the competition intensifies. However, maintaining these core principles becomes even more crucial at elite levels, where the mental and emotional demands on young athletes are greatest. By consistently reinforcing these values, parents can help their children navigate the challenges of high-level competition while developing into balanced, resilient individuals.

Seeking Professional Support and Taking a Pause

Seeking professional help, whether for yourself or your child, is not a sign of weakness or failure—it's a testament to your strength and commitment. Many sporting icons, from Lionel Messi to Serena Williams to Michael Jordan, have openly lauded the benefits of professional mental health support.

Consider Richard Williams, father of tennis legends Serena and Venus. Despite intense public pressure, he made the bold decision to delay his daughters' entry into professional tennis. Recognizing the paramount importance of their overall well-being over immediate athletic success, he chose to have them continue training and competing in amateur events. This strategy not only bolstered their self-confidence but also allowed them to hone critical athletic skills in a low-pressure environment.

More recently, gymnast Simone Biles made headlines when she withdrew from the 2020 Tokyo Olympics due to a mental health crisis. In the face of widespread criticism from news outlets, correspondents, social media, and even government figures, she made the courageous decision to step away from gymnastics entirely. Shortly after, news broke of the widespread abuse the U. S. women's gymnastics team had endured for years at the hands of their team doctor. It's entirely possible that the trauma Biles faced—both as a child of an addict and as a survivor of sexual abuse—resurfaced during the Olympics. Trauma, after all, has a way of shutting down the body.

But Biles's story didn't end there. She made a triumphant return at the 2024 Paris Olympics—well past what many considered her prime. After a year and a half of intensive therapy, she applied the tools and mechanisms learned in counseling to maintain her focus. The result? She clinched the all-around championship for the second time in her career and became the most decorated U. S. gymnast after leading her team to gold. Now a vocal advocate for mental health, Biles consistently emphasizes the critical importance of maintaining mental well-being as an athlete.

These stories underscore a crucial point: taking a step back, seeking help, and prioritizing mental health can lead to even greater achievements in the long run. It's not about giving up; it's about gearing up for future success.

Conclusion

Parenting an elite athlete is a complex, challenging, yet rewarding journey. By focusing on emotional support, open communication, and values-based parenting, you can nurture not just a successful athlete, but a well-rounded individual. Remember, your relationship with your child is more valuable than any trophy or contract. By implementing these strategies and maintaining a balanced, supportive approach, you play a crucial role in your child's athletic development and overall well-being.

For additional parenting resources, see the following:

- *The Sports Parent's Manual* by Dr. Jim Taylor
- *Mindset: The New Psychology of Success* by Carol S. Dweck
- *The Talent Code* by Daniel Coyle

These resources can provide further insights into supporting your child's athletic journey while maintaining a healthy parent-child relationship.

CHAPTER EIGHT

The Athlete and Emotional Cost

Richard Fowler and Holly Haynes

But we have this treasure in earthen vessels, that the excellence of the power may be of God and not of us. We are hard-pressed on every side, yet not crushed; we are perplexed, but not in despair; persecuted, but not forsaken; struck down, but not destroyed
—2 Corinthians 2:7-10, NKJV

Understanding Emotions and the Young Athlete

When we have family meetings with our children about sports, I am often told that "I don't understand" because I am not a competitive athlete. And that is true. I played music and competed throughout the city on piano and, later, violin. However, I do always tell my children that I understand competition well. Competition is key for elite athletes. They can thrive on it, but it can also be harmful. This chapter explores emotions and the young athlete. Parents may wish to take notes, however, as much of this information pertains to teens as a whole.

The world of youth sports is a complex arena where physical prowess meets emotional development. For many young athletes, their sport becomes more than just a pastime—it's a crucible where character is forged, dreams are pursued, and life lessons are learned. But with the thrill of competition and the joy of achievement come a host of emotional challenges that can shape a young person's experience in profound ways.

As we delve into this topic, it's crucial to remember that every young athlete's journey is unique. Some may find themselves on a fast track to success, while others may face a longer, more winding road. Regardless of the path, understanding and managing emotions play a pivotal role in not just athletic performance, but in overall well-being and personal growth.

Finding the Right Fit: Perseverance and Patience

Many younger athletes need a moment to develop within their sport before they reach the pinnacle of that sport. One thing professional athletes will tell you is that you must have perseverance and patience in order to make it through the long journey of becoming a professional athlete. But, even for athletes who plan to finish up their careers in college, the road to the college scholarship or offer to play can be very long and filled with ups and downs. So, what are the necessary characteristics of individual athletes and the emotions that may crop up along the way?

The path to athletic success is rarely a straight line. It's a journey marked by triumphs and setbacks, moments of brilliance, and periods of doubt. For young athletes, this journey can be particularly challenging as they navigate not just the physical demands of their sport, but also the emotional rollercoaster that comes with competition.

Perseverance, the ability to keep going in the face of obstacles, is a crucial trait for any athlete. It's what pushes them to get up early for training, to keep practicing when results aren't immediately visible, and to bounce back after a disappointing performance. Patience, on the other hand, is about understanding that progress takes time. It's the recognition that skills develop gradually, that setbacks are a natural part of the process, and that sometimes, the most significant growth happens during periods when outward progress seems slow.

These twin virtues—perseverance and patience—form the bedrock of athletic development. They allow young athletes to weather the storms of competition, to handle the pressures of expectation, and to maintain their passion for their sport even when faced with challenges.

But cultivating these traits isn't always easy. Young athletes may struggle with frustration when they don't see immediate results from their efforts. They might feel discouraged when comparing themselves to peers who seem to be progressing faster. They may even question their commitment to their sport during particularly tough periods.

This is where emotional intelligence comes into play. By developing an awareness of their emotions and learning strategies to manage them, young athletes can better navigate the ups and downs of their athletic journey. They can learn to channel frustration into motivation, view setbacks as learning opportunities, and maintain a sense of perspective even in the face of intense competition.

Cultivating Perseverance and Patience

Young athletes must cultivate perseverance and patience. This may mean participating in multiple sports before committing themselves to their primary sport. This approach, known as sports sampling, has been shown to have numerous benefits:

1. **Reduced burnout**: By engaging in various sports, athletes are less likely to experience mental and physical burnout from overspecialization.

2. **Improved overall athleticism**: Different sports develop different skills, contributing to a well-rounded athletic foundation.

3. **Enhanced decision-making**: Exposure to various sports scenarios improves an athlete's ability to read and react in game situations.

4. **Increased motivation**: Variety can keep young athletes engaged and excited about physical activity.

For example, many successful professional athletes were multisport athletes in their youth. LeBron James played football in high school before focusing on basketball. Abby Wambach, the former U. S. soccer star, played basketball and ran track. These experiences contributed to their overall athletic development and mental toughness. Dr. F. Stuart Sanders, a specialist in sports medicine (U. S. Olympic Figure Skating physician) echoes those examples by stating, "My advice to young athletes is to participate in several sports to enhance athletic skills and avoid burnout. Physically and skill wise, it is important for young athletes not to specialize early" (personal communication, November 22, 2023). The concept of sports sampling is more than just a way to prevent burnout or improve athleticism. It's a philosophy that recognizes the value of diverse experiences in shaping a young athlete's character and skills. By exposing themselves to different sports, young athletes learn to adapt to various situations, work with different types of teammates, and face a range of challenges.

This variety not only helps in developing a more well-rounded skill set but also provides valuable perspective. An athlete who has experienced different sports environments is less likely to become overly fixated on a single path to success. They understand that there are multiple ways to achieve goals and that skills learned in one area can often be applied in another.

Moreover, sports sampling can help young athletes discover their true passions. Some may find that they excel in a sport they never would have considered if they had specialized early. Others may confirm their love for their primary sport but gain valuable cross-training benefits from their other activities.

The patience required to explore different sports also translates well to the long-term development needed in any athletic pursuit. Athletes learn that progress isn't always linear and that skills developed in one area can unexpectedly benefit them in another.

It's important to note that while sports sampling has many benefits, it doesn't mean that focused training in a chosen sport isn't valuable. Rather, it suggests that early diversification can lead to more sustainable and enjoyable athletic careers in the long run. For parents and coaches, encouraging sports sampling may require patience of their own. It might mean resisting the urge to push for early specialization in the hope of gaining a competitive edge. Instead, the focus should be on fostering a love of physical activity and competition in general, trusting that this broader foundation will serve young athletes well as they progress in their athletic journeys.

However, in certain sports like gymnastics or figure skating, early specialization may be necessary to remain competitive at elite levels. In these cases, parents and coaches should consider encouraging participation in complementary activities outside of sports—such as music, art, or dance—that can provide similar benefits to multi-sport participation. These creative pursuits can help develop different neural pathways, enhance focus and discipline, and offer mental breaks from intense athletic training. Many successful gymnasts, for instance, have found that activities like piano or ballet complement their athletic training while providing valuable outlets for expression and stress relief.

The Role of Parents and Coaches in Helping Regulate Emotion

Parents should be aware of the various emotions that their athlete may express and when to provide extra support for the athlete. But, as athletes, they need to establish a relationship with a responsible adult so that they can address any issues they may be facing. In turn, adults need to learn to listen to the emotions of their athlete.

What might you miss as a parent because you are highly critical and need to discuss the errors of the child's most recent performance? In fact, parents can assess the mood of the player first. You will often learn about your child's level of competitiveness, self-esteem, and mood by trying to understand first.

The role of parents and coaches in a young athlete's life cannot be overstated. These adults serve as mentors, supporters, and guides through the complex world of competitive sports. However, it's crucial that they approach this role with sensitivity and emotional intelligence.

For parents, the line between supportive involvement and overbearing pressure can sometimes blur. It's natural to want the best for your child and to push them to excel. But it's equally important to recognize that your child's athletic journey is their own, and that your role is to support, not to control.

One of the most valuable things a parent can do is to create a safe emotional space for their young athlete. This means being a listener first and a critic second. After a game or competition, resist the urge to immediately launch into an analysis of what went wrong. Instead, tune into your child's emotional state. Are they frustrated? Disappointed? Excited? By acknowledging and validating their feelings first, you create an environment where they feel understood and supported.

This doesn't mean avoiding discussions about performance altogether. Rather, it's about timing and approach. When you do discuss areas for improvement, frame them in a constructive way that emphasizes learning and growth rather than failure or disappointment.

Coaches, too, play a crucial role in shaping a young athlete's emotional landscape. A good coach is not just a technical instructor but also an emotional mentor. They have the power to build an athlete's confidence or shatter it, to inspire perseverance or induce burnout.

Effective coaches recognize that each athlete is unique, not just in their physical abilities but in their emotional needs and motivations. They take the time to understand what drives each of their athletes, what their fears and aspirations are, and tailor their approach accordingly.

Strategies to Consider Implementing

Listen Actively
Focus on understanding your child's perspective before offering advice or criticism. This means giving them your full attention, asking open-ended questions, and reflecting back on what you hear to ensure you've understood correctly.

Provide Emotional Check-Ins

Regularly ask your child how they're feeling about their sport, not just about their performance. These check-ins can be informal conversations during car rides or over meals. The key is to create regular opportunities for your child to express their feelings about their athletic experience.

Celebrate Effort

Acknowledge the hard work and dedication, not just the outcomes. This helps to reinforce a growth mindset and reduces the pressure to achieve specific results. Praise can be as simple as, "I saw how hard you worked on your serve today," or "I'm impressed by how you kept your cool in that tough match."

Create a Safe Space

Ensure your child feels comfortable discussing their fears, anxieties, and frustrations without judgment. This might mean setting aside dedicated time for these conversations, away from siblings or other distractions. It also means responding to their concerns with empathy and understanding, even if you don't agree with their perspective.

Model Emotional Intelligence

Demonstrate healthy ways of dealing with disappointment, frustration, and success. Children often learn more from what we do than what we say, so be mindful of how you react to their performances and to challenges in your own life.

Encourage Self-Reflection

Help your young athlete develop the habit of reflecting on their own performance and emotions. You might ask questions like, "What did you learn from today's game?" or "How did you feel when you faced that challenging situation?"

Maintain Perspective

Remind your child (and yourself) that sports are just one part of life. Encourage other interests and emphasize the importance of balance. This can help reduce the pressure associated with athletic performance and provide a broader foundation for self-esteem.

Collaborate with Coaches

Maintain open communication with your child's coaches. Share insights about your child's emotional state or any concerns you may have and be open to hearing the coach's perspective. A united front between parents and coaches can provide consistent emotional support for the young athlete.

By implementing these strategies, parents and coaches can create an environment that nurtures not just athletic talent, but emotional resilience and overall well-being. Remember, the goal is not just to produce great athletes, but to help shape well-rounded individuals who can apply the lessons learned through sports to all aspects of their lives.

Work Hard, Stay Humble

Many athletes discuss the mantra of "work hard, stay humble" to improve their game. It is very important that athletes balance confidence with humility. Humility is not discussed enough in our modern world because it is often equated with weakness. However, it takes a pretty strong person to be humble. Humility is recognizing that one is not superior to another person—there is no innate superiority. Humility honors practice as key and allows for a growth mindset to develop in athletes because they know that they must continually work hard to move forward in their sport.

The phrase "work hard, stay humble" encapsulates a powerful philosophy that can guide young athletes through the ups and downs of their sporting careers. At its core, this mantra emphasizes the importance of balancing two crucial elements: the drive to excel and the wisdom to remain grounded.

Working hard is often celebrated in sports, and rightly so. It's the foundation of improvement, the engine that drives progress. Hard work means showing up for early morning practices, pushing through fatigue during training, and continually striving to refine skills and techniques. It's about setting goals and relentlessly pursuing them, even when progress seems slow, or setbacks occur.

But the "stay humble" part of the equation is equally important, though often overlooked. In a world that often celebrates individual achievement and self-promotion, humility can seem outdated or even counterproductive. Some might worry that being humble means downplaying their abilities or failing to assert themselves.

However, true humility is not about diminishing oneself. Rather, it's about maintaining a realistic and balanced view of one's abilities and achievements. It's the recognition that no matter how talented or successful an athlete becomes, there's always room for improvement. It's an acknowledgment that success is rarely, if ever, a solo endeavor–it's the result of support from coaches, teammates, family, and countless others.

Humility allows athletes to remain open to feedback and criticism, seeing these not as threats to their ego but as valuable tools for growth. It enables them to appreciate the talents of others, including their competitors, fostering a sense of respect and sportsmanship. Perhaps most importantly, humility provides a buffer against the pitfalls of success–the complacency, arrogance, or sense of entitlement that can derail even the most promising athletic careers.

For young athletes, cultivating this balance of hard work and humility can be challenging. The world of youth sports is often highly competitive, with pressure to stand out and prove oneself. Social media and increased visibility of young athletes can amplify this pressure, creating a temptation to focus on self-promotion rather than genuine self-improvement.

This is where the guidance of parents, coaches, and mentors becomes crucial. These adults can help young athletes understand that true confidence comes not from comparing oneself to others or seeking external validation, but from the knowledge of one's own efforts and improvements. They can teach that setbacks and failures are not signs of weakness, but opportunities for growth–and that how an athlete handles these challenges often says more about their character than their victories do. Practical ways to foster this "work hard, stay humble" mindset might include:

1. Encouraging athletes to set personal improvement goals rather than always focusing on outperforming others.

2. Teaching athletes to acknowledge and appreciate the contributions of teammates, coaches, and support staff.

3. Modeling humility by admitting mistakes and showing a willingness to learn and improve.

4. Celebrating effort and progress, not just results.

5. Encouraging athletes to engage in community service or mentoring younger players, fostering a sense of perspective and gratitude.

6. Teaching the value of sportsmanship and respect for opponents.

7. Helping athletes develop interests and identities outside of their sport, reducing the pressure to derive all self-worth from athletic performance.

By embracing the "work hard, stay humble" philosophy, young athletes can develop not just as competitors, but as individuals. They learn to take pride in their efforts and achievements without losing sight of the larger context. This balanced approach not only enhances their athletic performance but also prepares them for the challenges and opportunities they'll face beyond the world of sports.

The Power of a Growth Mindset

Dr. Carol Dweck's research on mindset has profound implications for athletes (2006). Those with a growth mindset believe that their abilities can be developed through dedication and hard work. This view creates a love of learning and a resilience that is essential for great accomplishment.

The concept of a growth mindset is particularly powerful in the realm of youth sports. It's an approach that can transform how young athletes view challenges, setbacks, and their own potential for improvement. At its core, a growth mindset is the belief that abilities and intelligence can be developed over time, rather than being fixed traits that one either has or doesn't have. For young athletes, adopting a growth mindset can lead to

1. Becoming more resilient: Setbacks are seen as opportunities to learn and improve, not as failures. When an

athlete with a growth mindset faces a defeat or a poor performance, they're more likely to view it as a temporary state and an opportunity to identify areas for improvement. Rather than becoming discouraged, they become motivated to work harder and try new strategies.

2.   Putting forth greater effort: Understanding that effort leads to mastery encourages harder work. Athletes with a growth mindset are more likely to put in extra hours of practice, knowing that their efforts will pay off in improved performance. They understand that talent alone is not enough – it's the combination of talent and dedicated effort that leads to success.

3.   Embracing challenges: Difficult tasks are seen as chances to grow, not threats to avoid. Instead of shying away from tough opponents or new skills that seem daunting, growth-minded athletes actively seek out these challenges. They understand that pushing beyond their comfort zone is where real growth happens.

4.   Learning from criticism: Feedback is viewed as valuable information for improvement, not as personal attacks. Athletes with a growth mindset are more open to constructive criticism from coaches and teammates. They're able to separate their performance from their self-worth, allowing them to process feedback without feeling threatened or discouraged.

Cultivating a growth mindset in young athletes requires consistent effort from coaches, parents, and the athletes themselves. Here are some strategies to foster this mindset:

1.   Praise effort and strategy, not just results: Instead of focusing solely on wins or losses, commend the hard work, perseverance, and smart strategies employed by the athlete. This helps shift the focus from outcomes to the process of improvement.

2.   Encourage risk-taking and learning from mistakes: Create an environment where it's okay to make mistakes as long as athletes are willing to learn from them.

Celebrate attempts at new skills or strategies, even if they don't immediately lead to success.

3. Use the power of "yet": When an athlete says they can't do something, encourage them to add "yet" to the end of the sentence. This simple word can shift their perspective from a fixed state to one of potential growth.

4. Share stories of growth: Provide examples of famous athletes who improved dramatically through hard work and perseverance. These stories can inspire young athletes and reinforce the idea that abilities can be developed over time.

5. Set process goals: While outcome goals (like winning a championship) are important, also encourage athletes to set process goals that focus on personal improvement. These might include mastering a specific skill, improving a particular aspect of their game, or consistently putting in a certain amount of practice time.

6. Teach the science of skill development: Help athletes understand how practice and repetition physically change their brains and bodies. This knowledge can reinforce the idea that improvement is always possible with the right effort and approach.

7. Model a growth mindset: As a coach or parent, demonstrate your own commitment to learning and improvement. Be open about your own challenges and how you work to overcome them.

8. Create a team culture of growth: In team sports, encourage athletes to support each other's growth. Celebrate team members who show significant improvement, not just the top performers.

9. Use reflective practices: Encourage athletes to regularly reflect on their progress, challenges, and strategies for improvement. This can be done through journaling, team discussions, or one-on-one conversations with coaches.

10. Emphasize the joy of the process: Help athletes find enjoyment in the process of improvement itself, not just

in achieving specific outcomes. This can lead to a more sustainable and fulfilling athletic experience.

By fostering a growth mindset, we equip young athletes with a powerful tool that extends far beyond their sporting endeavors. This mindset can positively impact their academic pursuits, future careers, and overall approach to life's challenges. It instills a love of learning and a resilience that will serve them well in all aspects of their lives. Moreover, a growth mindset aligns perfectly with the "work hard, stay humble" philosophy discussed earlier. It encourages hard work by reinforcing the link between effort and improvement, while also promoting humility by acknowledging that there's always room for growth and learning.

For young athletes navigating the complex world of competitive sports, a growth mindset can be a game-changer. It can transform the way they view challenges, handle setbacks, and approach their own potential. By embracing this mindset, athletes can not only enhance their performance but also develop a more positive and empowering relationship with their sport.

Balancing Confidence and Humility

While it's crucial for athletes to believe in their abilities, an overinflated ego can be detrimental. Here's how to strike the right balance:

1. Acknowledge teammates: Recognize that success is often a team effort, even in individual sports.

2. Learn from others: Be open to advice and criticism from coaches, teammates, and even opponents.

3. Stay grounded: Remember that there's always room for improvement, no matter how successful you become.

4. Practice gratitude: Regularly express appreciation for the opportunities and support you receive.

The delicate balance between confidence and humility is a key factor in an athlete's success and personal growth. Confidence is essential—it's what allows athletes to perform under pressure, to take risks, and to push their limits. However, unchecked confidence can easily turn into arrogance, which can be detrimental to both individual performance and team dynamics.

Humility, on the other hand, keeps an athlete grounded and open to growth. It fosters a team-first mentality and helps maintain perspective in both victory and defeat. But too much humility, or false humility, can undermine an athlete's self-belief and hold them back from reaching their full potential. So how can young athletes cultivate this balance? Let's delve deeper into the strategies mentioned.

Acknowledge Teammates

In team sports, it's crucial to recognize that success is a collective effort. Even in seemingly individual moments of brilliance, there are often unseen contributions from teammates–the perfect pass that led to a goal, the defensive play that created a scoring opportunity, or the words of encouragement that boosted morale. By acknowledging these contributions, athletes not only foster a positive team environment but also gain a more realistic view of their own role in the team's success. Even in individual sports, athletes can practice this by recognizing the support of their coaches, training partners, family members, and others who contribute to their success. This acknowledgment helps maintain humility while also strengthening the support network that's crucial for long-term success.

Learn from Others

Being open to advice and criticism is a hallmark of both humility and a growth mindset. It requires setting aside ego and recognizing that everyone–coaches, teammates, and even opponents–can offer valuable insights. This openness to learning is a sign of true confidence. It shows that an athlete is secure enough in their abilities to acknowledge areas for improvement. Encourage young athletes to actively seek feedback, not just from authority figures like coaches, but also from peers. Sometimes, a teammate might notice something that a coach misses. Even opponents can be sources of learning–analyzing how they play, their strategies, and their skills can provide valuable lessons.

Stay Grounded

Success can be intoxicating, especially for young athletes experiencing it for the first time. It's important to help them maintain perspective. This doesn't mean downplaying achievements but rather framing them as part of an ongoing journey of improvement. One effective way to stay grounded is to always have new goals on the horizon. After achieving one milestone, encourage athletes to set their sights on the next challenge. This keeps them focused on growth rather than resting on their laurels. Another strategy is to regularly reflect on the journey so far–the challenges overcome, the lessons learned, and the people who have helped along the way. This reflection can foster a sense of gratitude and humility, even in the face of significant success.

Practice Gratitude

Gratitude is a powerful tool for maintaining both humility and positivity. It shifts focus from what an athlete might feel entitled to, to what they're fortunate to have. This can include opportunities to compete, access to training facilities, support from family and coaches, good health, and more. Encourage young athletes to make gratitude a regular practice. This could be through a gratitude journal, where they write down things they're thankful for each day. Or it could be through verbal expressions of appreciation to coaches, teammates, and supporters. Gratitude can also extend to the sport itself–appreciating the joy of playing, the lessons learned through competition, and the personal growth facilitated by athletic pursuits. This appreciation can help maintain enthusiasm and commitment, even during challenging times.

By implementing these strategies, young athletes can develop a balanced approach that combines self-belief with openness to growth and appreciation for others. This balance not only enhances athletic performance but also contributes to personal development and positive relationships both in and out of sports.

Remember, confidence and humility are not fixed traits, but skills that can be developed over time. With consistent effort and guidance, young athletes can learn to navigate this balance, setting themselves up for success in their sport and in life beyond athletics.

Perfection vs. Excellence

Another key emotional understanding of elite athletes is the role of perfection and excellence. Many times, players will practice their sport over and over again—with the hope that they will become perfect at their craft. However, many sports are not about being perfect—for that is impossible. They are about learning to quickly cope with mistakes and continue to perform at a high level. Mistakes often teach concepts. Failure to score a goal or missed baskets can have an impact on a game, but an emotionally secure player understands that they may have to make in-game adjustments to improve their chances of scoring. They do not simply give up—they adjust.

The pursuit of perfection is a common trap that many young athletes fall into. It's an understandable desire—after all, who doesn't want to perform flawlessly? But this pursuit can often lead to negative outcomes that hinder both performance and enjoyment of the sport.

The Pitfalls of Perfectionism

While striving for excellence can be motivating, perfectionism often leads to negative outcomes. Performance anxiety is one of the most common consequences. The fear of making mistakes can paralyze athletes, leading to underperformance. When an athlete is overly focused on avoiding errors, they often become tense and hesitant. This tension can interfere with the fluid, automatic movements that are crucial for peak performance in most sports. Moreover, the fear of making mistakes can prevent athletes from taking necessary risks or trying new strategies that could potentially improve their game.

Another significant drawback is decreased enjoyment. When the focus is solely on flawless execution, the joy of playing can be lost. Sports, at their core, should be enjoyable. The pressure to be perfect can turn what was once a source of joy into a source of stress and anxiety. This loss of enjoyment can lead to burnout and potentially cause talented young athletes to leave their sport altogether.

Burnout represents a serious consequence of perfectionism in athletics. Constant self-criticism and the pressure to be perfect can lead to mental and physical exhaustion. Perfectionists often have difficulty acknowledging when they've done "enough." They may overtrain, skip rest days, or push through injuries—all in pursuit of an unattainable ideal. This relentless drive can lead to both physical and emotional burnout.

Perhaps most concerning for long-term athletic development is stunted growth. Fear of failure can prevent athletes from taking risks and learning new skills. Growth often comes from stepping out of one's comfort zone and trying new things. However, a perfectionist mindset can keep athletes stuck in their current skill set, afraid to attempt new techniques or strategies for fear of not executing them perfectly.

Embracing Excellence

For many young athletes, shifting from a focus on perfection to excellence allows them to make those in-game adjustments. By having a mindset of excellence, athletes seek to do their very best in every game. Mistakes often do not shut down these types of players because they enter a game or match less focused on their individual performance and more so on that of the team. In individual sports, athletes do not focus as much on the details of their performance as on the outcomes of their hard work. They can adapt in difficult situations.

The key difference between perfection and excellence lies in the approach. Perfection is an unattainable standard that focuses on flawless execution. Excellence, on the other hand, is about consistent high performance, continuous improvement, and the ability to adapt and overcome challenges. Dr. Hannah Elizabeth Jones, former elite gymnast, says that athletes should "keep a tight mind":

> This quote means a lot to me. These four words have gotten me through many challenges both inside and outside of the gym. Having a tight mind means blocking out all outside thoughts. It is similar to a meditative state. Whenever I am in pain during our conditioning sessions, I would shut off my mind and ignore every voice telling me that what I am going through is hard. Acquiring and refining this mental ability will keep you on track, focused, and impenetrable (personal

communication).

The Benefits of Embracing Excellence for Young Athletes

Resilience. Athletes focused on excellence are better equipped to handle setbacks. They see mistakes as learning opportunities rather than failures, allowing them to bounce back quickly from disappointments.

Adaptability. An excellent mindset promotes flexibility. These athletes can adjust their strategies mid-game or mid-season, responding effectively to new challenges or unexpected situations.

Continuous Improvement. Rather than chasing an impossible standard of perfection, athletes striving for excellence are always looking for ways to get better. This leads to steady, sustainable progress over time.

Better Teamwork. In team sports, an excellent mindset promotes better cooperation. Athletes are less likely to blame teammates for mistakes and more likely to work together to overcome challenges.

Increased Confidence. Paradoxically, letting go of the need to be perfect can boost an athlete's confidence. They trust in their ability to handle whatever comes their way, rather than fearing potential mistakes.

Strategies for Cultivating a Mindset of Excellence

Set Process Goals. Focus on controllable aspects of performance rather than just outcomes. For example, instead of setting a goal to "win every game," an athlete might aim to "improve free throw accuracy by 10% this season" or "execute our team's defensive strategy consistently."

Celebrate Progress. Acknowledge improvements, no matter how small. This reinforces the idea that growth is ongoing and that every step forward is valuable. Coaches and parents can play a crucial role here by pointing out improvements that the athlete might not notice themselves.

Learn from Mistakes. Analyze errors as opportunities for growth rather than failures. After a game or competition, encourage athletes to reflect on what went well, what could be improved, and what they learned. This turns mistakes from sources of shame into valuable learning experiences.

Visualize Success. Use mental imagery to picture successful performances, including overcoming obstacles. This technique can help athletes prepare for challenges and build confidence in their ability to handle difficult situations.

Practice Self-Compassion. Teach athletes to treat themselves with the same kindness they would offer a teammate who made a mistake. Self-compassion can help buffer against the negative effects of errors and maintain motivation.

Focus on the Present. Encourage athletes to stay focused on the current moment rather than worrying about past mistakes or future outcomes. Mindfulness techniques can be helpful here.

Emphasize Effort and Growth. Praise athletes for their hard work, perseverance, and improvement rather than just their natural talents or victories.

Remember the importance of shifting from a perfectionistic mindset to one focused on excellence. This change can help young athletes improve their performance and enjoy their athletic journey more fully. Embracing challenges, adapting to difficulties, and continually striving for improvement are valuable skills that will serve athletes well both in sports and in life beyond athletics. Dr. Hannah Jones provides the following steps for successful athletes:

1. **Push yourself**. You can always do more than you think you can. Whenever you believe that you are at your stopping point, push for 10% more. I guarantee you can do it. Once you do, you will begin to realize that the only limits you have are set by yourself.

2. **Always have a goal in mind**. To keep moving forward and continue improving, you need to always have your eye on a goal. Once you reach a goal, be proud of yourself. Then, immediately set another. This is true for anything in life. Each day is an opportunity for improvement, but we will stay stagnant if we never set goals for ourselves.

3. **Do it to prove to yourself that you can**. For most athletes, competitiveness is second nature and while

winning does feel good, that is not the only thing you should be training for. There is nothing more empowering than putting in hours upon hours of blood, sweat, and tears and then earning a place on the podium. True hard work does pay off. It becomes a powerful cycle of showing yourself how much you can do.

This approach aligns well with the growth mindset we discussed earlier. It encourages athletes to see their abilities as developable through effort and learning, rather than as fixed traits. It also complements the balance of confidence and humility, allowing athletes to believe in their abilities while remaining open to growth and improvement.

The goal isn't to lower standards or accept mediocrity. Instead, it's about setting high but achievable standards that promote growth, resilience, and long-term success. By embracing excellence over perfection, young athletes can unlock their full potential while maintaining their love for their sport.

The Role of Emotions in Sports Performance

Understanding and managing emotions is crucial for athletic success. Here's a deeper look at how emotions impact performance and strategies for emotional regulation:

The Impact of Emotions on Performance

Emotional Intelligence and Resilience

By implementing emotional regulation strategies, young athletes can develop greater emotional intelligence and resilience, enhancing their athletic performance and equipping them with valuable life skills. Understanding the connection between emotions and athletic performance is essential. Athletes often experience being "in the zone" when they achieve optimal arousal and everything falls into place. Conversely, they may also encounter times when they feel either too relaxed and unmotivated or too anxious and tense to perform at their best.

The key is to find the right balance, which varies between athletes and sports. For instance, a golfer putting for a championship might require a lower level of arousal to maintain steady hands and focus, while a sprinter at the starting blocks might benefit from a higher level of arousal to explode out of the gates.

Emotional Contagion

Emotions can spread within a team. A single player's positive or negative emotions can influence the entire group's performance. This phenomenon is particularly crucial in team sports but can also impact individual athletes who are part of a larger team or training group. A teammate's enthusiasm can be infectious, lifting the spirits and performance of the entire team. On the flip side, one player's frustration or negativity can create a ripple effect, potentially derailing the team's focus and cohesion.

Understanding emotional contagion can assist athletes in being more conscious of how their own emotions may be impacting their teammates, highlighting the significance of team leaders who can uphold a positive emotional state even in challenging circumstances.

Decision-Making

Strong emotions can impair judgment and lead to poor in-game decisions. During competitive events, emotions can run high, impacting performance. While passion and intensity can enhance performance, uncontrolled emotions can cloud judgment. An angry player might make overly aggressive moves, risking fouls or injuries. Similarly, a frustrated athlete may deviate from the game plan in favor of risky individual plays, while fear could lead a player to hesitate when quick action is needed.

Teaching young athletes to recognize and manage their emotions can significantly improve their decision-making abilities under pressure. This does not mean suppressing emotions entirely but rather learning to channel them productively.

Physical Performance

Emotions can impact physical performance through changes in muscle tension, breathing rate, and hormonal responses. The mind-body connection is powerful in sports. Anxiety can cause muscles to tense up, impairing fluid movement and reducing power. It can also lead to shallow, rapid breathing, which can negatively impact endurance. On the other hand, positive emotions like excitement can trigger the release of adrenaline, potentially enhancing strength and speed.

Understanding these physical responses can help athletes learn to use their emotions to their advantage or at least mitigate negative physical effects.

Strategies for Emotional Regulation

Mindfulness

Practicing mindfulness can help athletes stay present and focused, rather than getting caught up in anxiety about the future or regret about past mistakes. Mindfulness involves paying attention to the present moment without judgment. For athletes, this can mean focusing on the feel of their movements, the sound of their breath, or the texture of the ball or equipment they're using. Regular mindfulness practice can help athletes develop the ability to notice their thoughts and emotions without getting carried away by them.

This skill can be particularly valuable in high-pressure situations. An athlete who has practiced mindfulness might be able to notice feelings of anxiety arising without getting caught up in them, allowing them to refocus on the task at hand.

Controlled Breathing

Techniques like box breathing or diaphragmatic breathing can help manage stress and anxiety in high-pressure situations. Breathing is one of the few autonomic functions that we can consciously control, making it a powerful tool for emotional regulation. Controlled breathing can help lower the heart rate, reduce muscle tension, and promote a sense of calm.

Box breathing (inhaling for a count of four, holding for four, exhaling for four, and holding for four) is one technique that athletes can use to quickly center themselves. Diaphragmatic breathing, which involves deep belly breaths, can be practiced regularly to promote overall relaxation and stress management.

Positive Self-Talk

Replacing negative thoughts with positive, encouraging self-talk can boost confidence and performance. The internal dialogue that athletes maintain can significantly impact their emotional state and, consequently, their performance. Negative self-talk ("I'm going to mess this up") can increase anxiety and decrease confidence. On the other hand, positive self-talk ("I've practiced this countless times, I can do it") can enhance confidence and focus.

Teaching young athletes to recognize their self-talk patterns and consciously shift towards more positive, constructive internal dialogue can be a game-changer. This doesn't mean ignoring problems or pretending everything is perfect, but rather framing challenges in a way that feels manageable and motivating.

Visualization

As mentioned in previous chapters, mental rehearsal of successful performances can help manage emotions and improve actual performance. Visualization, or mental imagery, is a powerful tool used by many elite athletes. By mentally rehearsing a performance–including the sights, sounds, and physical sensations involved–athletes can build confidence, reduce anxiety, and improve their actual performance.

Importantly, effective visualization isn't just about picturing perfect performances. It should also include visualizing how to handle challenges or mistakes. This can help athletes feel more prepared and less anxious about potential setbacks.

Routine Development

Pre-performance routines can help athletes enter an optimal emotional state for competition. Consistent routines can serve as emotional anchors, helping athletes feel grounded and focused regardless of the circumstances. These routines might include specific warm-up exercises, visualization practices, or even seemingly unrelated rituals (like always putting on the left shoe first).

The key is that these routines are consistent and controllable, providing a sense of familiarity and calm even in high-pressure situations. They can help trigger the optimal emotional state for performance, almost like a conditioned response.

By understanding the role of emotions in sports performance and implementing these emotional regulation strategies, young athletes can develop greater emotional intelligence and resilience. This not only enhances their athletic performance but also equips them with valuable life skills that extend far beyond the playing field.

Remember, emotional regulation is a skill that requires practice, just like any physical technique. Encourage young athletes to incorporate these strategies into their regular training routines, not just during competitions. With time and consistent effort, they can learn to harness their emotions as a powerful tool for peak performance.

The Importance of Mental Health in Athletics

While physical health is often prioritized in sports, mental health is equally crucial for long-term success and well-being. Here's why mental health matters and how to support it:

The Mental Health Challenges Athletes Face

Performance Pressure
The constant need to perform at a high level can lead to anxiety and stress. Young athletes often face immense pressure to succeed, whether it's from coaches, parents, teammates, or themselves. This pressure can be particularly intense in high-stakes situations like championship games or tryouts for elite teams. Over time, this constant stress can take a toll on an athlete's mental health, potentially leading to anxiety disorders or burnout.

It's important to recognize that some degree of pressure can be motivating, but excessive or constant pressure can be detrimental. Athletes may begin to tie their self-worth entirely to their athletic performance, creating a fragile sense of identity that's vulnerable to setbacks.

Identity Issues
When an athlete's self-worth is too closely tied to their athletic performance, it can lead to identity crises, especially during slumps or after retirement. Many young athletes, especially those who have been successful from an early age, may begin to define themselves primarily as athletes. While passion for a sport is

positive, an overly narrow identity can be problematic. When an athlete's entire sense of self is wrapped up in their sport, poor performance or injuries can be devastating.

This issue often comes to a head when athletes face retirement, whether due to age, injury, or other factors. The transition out of competitive sports can be extremely challenging for those who have never developed identities outside of their athletic pursuits.

Body Image Concerns

In sports where body type is emphasized, athletes may develop unhealthy relationships with food and exercise. Certain sports place a high premium on specific body types or weights. Wrestlers may feel pressure to cut weight drastically, gymnasts might feel they need to delay puberty to maintain a certain body type, and runners might feel pressure to be as lean as possible. These pressures can lead to disordered eating patterns, over-exercise, and negative body image.

It's crucial to promote a healthy relationship with food and exercise, emphasizing performance and health over appearance. Athletes should be educated about proper nutrition for their sport and the dangers of extreme dieting or overtraining.

Burnout

The demanding nature of competitive sports can lead to physical and emotional exhaustion. Burnout is a state of physical, emotional, and mental exhaustion that can occur when athletes feel overwhelmed by the demands of their sport. It often happens when there's an imbalance between the effort put into training and competing and the rewards or results achieved.

Signs of burnout might include loss of enthusiasm for the sport, decreased performance despite continued training, mood changes, and physical symptoms like persistent fatigue or frequent injuries. Burnout can be particularly insidious because it often develops gradually over time.

Supporting Athletes' Mental Health

Normalize Mental Health Discussions

Create an environment where it's okay to talk about mental health challenges. One of the biggest barriers to addressing mental health issues in sports is the stigma that often surrounds them. Many athletes fear being seen as weak if they admit to struggling mentally. To combat this, it's crucial to create a culture where mental health is viewed as an integral part of overall health and performance.

Coaches and team leaders can play a key role in this by openly discussing the importance of mental health, sharing their own experiences if comfortable, and treating mental health concerns with the same seriousness as physical injuries. Regular check-ins about mental well-being should be as normal as asking about physical condition.

Provide Access to Mental Health Professionals

Ensure athletes have access to sports psychologists or counselors. Just as teams have physical trainers and physiotherapists, they should also have mental health professionals available. These could be sports psychologists who understand the unique pressures of athletics, or general mental health counselors. It's important that seeking help from these professionals is seen as a normal and positive step, not a last resort. Some teams have found success in making regular check-ins with mental health professionals a standard part of their program for all athletes.

Promote Work-Life Balance

Encourage interests and activities outside of sports. While dedication to one's sport is admirable, it is crucial for athletes to develop interests and identities outside of athletics. This not only provides a mental break from the pressures of competition but also helps build a more well-rounded identity that can withstand the ups and downs of an athletic career. Encourage young athletes to pursue hobbies, maintain friendships outside of their sport, and keep up with their studies. This balance can actually enhance athletic performance by reducing stress and preventing burnout.

Educate About Mental Health

Provide information about common mental health issues and coping strategies. Many young athletes may not recognize the signs of mental health issues or know how to address them. Providing education about common concerns like anxiety, depression, and eating disorders can help athletes identify potential problems early.

This education should also cover positive mental health practices, such as stress management techniques, the importance of sleep, and healthy ways to handle pressure and disappointment.

Monitor for Warning Signs

Be aware of changes in behavior, mood, or performance that might indicate mental health concerns. Coaches, parents, and teammates should be educated about the warning signs of mental health issues. These might include sudden changes in mood or behavior, decreased performance despite continued training, social withdrawal, changes in eating or sleeping habits, or expressed feelings of hopelessness or worthlessness.

If these signs are observed, it's important to approach the athlete with concern and support, and to connect them with appropriate professional help if needed.

By prioritizing mental health alongside physical health, we can help ensure that young athletes not only perform at their best but also develop the resilience and emotional intelligence to thrive both in and out of sports. Remember, a mentally healthy athlete is more likely to enjoy their sport, perform consistently, and have a positive impact on their team and community.

The journey of a young athlete is filled with both physical and emotional challenges. By understanding these challenges and implementing supportive strategies, we can help create an environment where athletes can thrive, grow, and reach their full potential. This holistic approach to athlete development not only enhances sports performance but also equips young people with valuable life skills that will serve them well long after their competitive careers have ended.

Perseverance Revisited

As discussed at the beginning of the chapter, perseverance is key for the elite athlete. Keep going. There is a finish line. It may not look exactly as you expected.

Perseverance is often what separates good athletes from great ones. It's the ability to keep pushing forward, even when faced with obstacles, setbacks, or failures. For young athletes, developing this quality can be challenging, but it's essential for long-term success both in sports and in life.

Let's delve deeper into the concept of perseverance and how it applies to the journey of a young athlete:

Embracing the Process

Perseverance isn't just about gritting your teeth and pushing through hardship. It's about embracing the entire process of athletic development, including the ups and downs. Young athletes need to understand that progress isn't always linear. There will be periods of rapid improvement, plateaus, and even temporary setbacks. The key is to stay committed to the long-term goal, even when short-term results are disappointing.

Redefining Success

Part of perseverance is being able to redefine what success looks like. For a young athlete, success might initially be defined as winning every game or being the best on the team. As they mature, it's important to shift this definition to focus more on personal growth and improvement. Did you give your best effort? Did you learn something new? Did you support your teammates? These can all be measures of success that encourage perseverance.

Learning from Setbacks

Perseverance doesn't mean never failing; it means learning how to bounce back from failure. Encourage young athletes to view setbacks as learning opportunities. After a loss or a poor performance, guide them through a reflective process: What went wrong? What can be improved? How can this experience make you a better athlete?

The Power of Yet

Introduce the concept of "yet" to young athletes. When they say, "I can't do this," encourage them to add "yet" to the end of the sentence. This simple word can shift their perspective from a fixed mindset to a growth mindset, reminding them that with perseverance, they can improve and overcome challenges.

Celebrating Small Wins

While it's important to have big, long-term goals, perseverance is often sustained by acknowledging and celebrating small wins along the way. Did an athlete master a new skill they've been struggling with? Did they improve their time, even if by just a small margin? Recognizing these achievements can provide the motivation to keep going.

Building Mental Toughness

Perseverance and mental toughness go hand in hand. Mental toughness is about maintaining focus and determination in the face of adversity. It can be developed through practices like visualization, positive self-talk, and mindfulness. Encourage athletes to incorporate these techniques into their regular training routines.

The Role of Support Systems

No athlete perseveres alone. The support of coaches, teammates, family, and friends is crucial. Teach young athletes the importance of leaning on their support system during tough times. At the same time, encourage them to be supportive of others, creating a culture of perseverance within their team or training group.

Balancing Perseverance and Self-Care

While perseverance is crucial, it's equally important to teach young athletes when to take a step back. Pushing through minor discomfort is one thing, but ignoring serious pain or extreme mental stress can lead to injury or burnout. Help athletes learn to distinguish between challenges they should push through and signs that they need to rest or seek help.

Perseverance Beyond Sports

The perseverance developed through athletics can serve young people well in all areas of life. Encourage athletes to apply the same determination they show in sports to their academics, personal relationships, and future careers. This can help them see the broader value of the qualities they're developing through their athletic pursuits.

The Unexpected Finish Line

As the introduction to this section notes, there is a finish line, but it may not look exactly as expected. This is an important lesson in perseverance. Sometimes, despite our best efforts, things don't work out exactly as we hoped. An injury might end an athletic career earlier than planned, or an athlete might realize their passion lies in a different area.

True perseverance includes the ability to adapt to these unexpected outcomes. It's about taking the skills, discipline, and resilience developed through athletics and applying them to new challenges and opportunities. The "finish line" might not be an Olympic medal or a professional contract, but rather the development of character, skills, and experiences that will serve the athlete well throughout their life.

In conclusion, perseverance is not just about never giving up. It's about approaching challenges with a growth mindset, learning from setbacks, celebrating progress, and staying committed to long-term development. By fostering perseverance in young athletes, we prepare them not just for success in sports, but for the many challenges and opportunities they'll face throughout their lives.

Remember, the journey of an athlete is as important as the destination. By embracing perseverance, young athletes can ensure that regardless of where their athletic pursuits lead them, they'll emerge stronger, more resilient, and better prepared for whatever life throws their way.

The Long-Term View of Athletic Development

It's essential for young athletes and their support systems to understand that athletic development is a long-term process. Here are some key points to remember:

Individual Timelines

Every athlete develops at their own pace. Early success doesn't guarantee long-term achievement, and late bloomers can still reach great heights. This point cannot be overstressed in youth athletics. Too often, there's a tendency to identify "star" athletes at a young age, lavishing them with attention and resources while overlooking others who may simply be on a different developmental timeline.

Physical development plays a huge role here. Some children may hit growth spurts earlier than others, giving them a temporary advantage in size and strength. However, these early advantages don't necessarily translate to long-term success. Conversely, athletes who are smaller or less physically developed in their early teens may catch up or even surpass their peers later on.

Cognitive and emotional development also occur at different rates. An athlete who struggles with complex strategies or handling pressure at 12 might excel in these areas by 16. The key is to create an environment that allows for these varied timelines. Coaches and parents should focus on individual progress rather than constantly comparing athletes to their peers. This approach can help prevent talented "late bloomers" from becoming discouraged and dropping out before they've had a chance to reach their potential.

Embracing the Process

Focus on continuous improvement rather than immediate results. In a world that often celebrates instant gratification, embracing the long-term process of athletic development can be challenging. However, it's essential for sustainable success and enjoyment of sport.

Encourage young athletes to set both short-term and long-term goals. Short-term goals provide motivation and a sense of accomplishment along the way, while long-term goals give direction to their overall development. Emphasize the importance of consistent effort over time. Help athletes understand that small, consistent improvements can lead to significant progress over months and years. This might involve keeping a training log or regularly video recording performances to track progress visually.

Celebrate effort and personal improvement as much as (or more than) competitive results. An athlete who finishes last but achieves a personal best time has made significant progress in their development; even if it's not reflected in their placing.

Adapting to Changes

As athletes grow and develop, their strengths and weaknesses may change. Be prepared to adjust training and expectations accordingly. Physical changes during adolescence can significantly impact an athlete's performance and capabilities. A gymnast who excelled as a small, light child may struggle as they grow taller and heavier. A swimmer who was average might suddenly excel after a growth spurt increases their arm span.

These changes can be frustrating for young athletes who may feel like they're losing ground or struggling with skills they once found easy. It's important to help them understand that these changes are normal and temporary. Encourage patience and persistence as they adapt to their changing bodies.

Mental and emotional changes are equally important. As athletes mature, they may develop new interests or shift their priorities. They might become more (or less) competitive or develop a deeper understanding of strategy in their sport.

Coaches and parents should be flexible, ready to adjust training methods, positions, or even sports to align with the athlete's changing abilities and interests. This might mean allowing a previously specialized athlete to try other sports, or helping a multi-sport athlete focus on the one where they're showing the most promise and enjoyment.

Learning from Setbacks

Injuries, losses, and disappointments are part of the journey. Use these experiences as opportunities for growth and learning. Setbacks are inevitable in any athletic career. How an athlete responds to these challenges can often define their long-term success and enjoyment of their sport.

Injuries, while unfortunate, can be opportunities for athletes to develop mental toughness, explore cross-training options, and gain a deeper appreciation for their sport. Encourage injured athletes to stay involved with their team, focus on the aspects of training they can do (like mental preparation or a study strategy), and use the recovery process as a chance to come back stronger.

Losses and disappointments, while painful in the moment, are often where the most significant learning occurs. After a defeat, guide athletes through a reflective process: What went well? What could be improved? What can be learned from this experience? This approach turns losses into valuable learning opportunities.

It's also important to help athletes maintain perspective. A single loss or a bad season doesn't define their entire athletic career. Many of the world's top athletes have stories of significant setbacks that ultimately contributed to their success.

Long-term athletic development is about more than just physical training and skill acquisition. It's a holistic process that involves physical, mental, and emotional growth. By taking a long-term view, we can help young athletes navigate the ups and downs of their sporting journey, maximizing their potential for success and, more importantly, their enjoyment of and personal growth through sport.

Remember, the ultimate goal of youth sports isn't just to produce elite athletes, but to foster healthy, well-rounded individuals who can apply the lessons learned through athletics to all aspects of their lives. By embracing this long-term perspective, we can help ensure that sports remain a positive, enriching experience for young people, regardless of where their athletic journey ultimately leads them.

CHAPTER NINE

The Coach and Emotional Cost

Stacy Hall

Coaching: The Roller Coaster of Emotions

Coaching is an incredibly demanding profession that carries enormous pressure. These field generals are expected to get everything right, all the time, while performing in the public eye. Even when their team wins, criticism often follows because they didn't win by enough or made perceived mistakes. Yet, coaching can also be one of the most rewarding professions on the planet. The opportunity to invest in young people, help them, teach them, develop them, and watch them flourish as they reach their full potential is indeed life changing. As the famous evangelist Billy Graham once said, "A coach will impact more people in one year than the average person will in an entire lifetime" (as cited in Rennicke, 2014). This statement encapsulates both the incredible opportunity and the intimidating responsibility that comes with coaching.

Coaches are, by nature, competitors. They want to win! Most coaches thrive on competition, working longer and harder knowing that their competitors are also striving to defeat them. This competitiveness, combined with the responsibility to develop players and to meet the expectations of parents, administrators, and fans, can create enormous waves of emotions. One second, coaches can feel like they're riding on a cloud; in the next second, they can spiral into a pit of misery. How coaches handle their own emotions and how they're able to regulate the emotions of their athletes can be the difference between a good coach and a great one.

The Multifaceted Nature of Coaching

Any moderately successful coach must have a baseline knowledge of the X's and O's of their respective sport. This means understanding the basic rules and strategy of the game. They also need to possess excellent time management and communication skills, and at certain levels, they need to be good recruiters and administrators. However, another vital element required of great coaches is the ability to manage emotions.

This chapter examines the emotions involved with coaching in three primary areas:

1. The impact emotion has on coaching
2. The importance of emotional intelligence
3. Emotional exhaustion

The more coaches understand and improve in these areas, the more effective they will be, and ultimately, the more successful their program will become.

The Impact of Emotion on Coaching

In 2019, a significant research article was published in *The Sport Journal* entitled "The Role of Emotion in Sport Coaching: A Review of the Literature" by Eric Magrum and Bryan McCullick. The article reviewed 23 peer-reviewed articles related to the keywords *emotion* and *coaching*. The authors discovered through their analysis that each of the articles could be categorized into one of four groups, examining how emotion plays a role in coach effectiveness, coach-athlete interaction, development of emotional intelligence, and navigating job-related stress, pressure, and burnout. This review article underscored what much research already tells us—coaches are more effective when they can recognize and comprehend their own emotions, as well as those of others, and understand the probable after-effects of their interactions. In general, emotional competence is an essential skill for effective coaching.

Coach Effectiveness and Emotion

Magrum and McCullick (2019) effectively illustrate how high-caliber coaches have determined that their ability to connect emotionally with their players was a crucial factor in their coaching. "Therefore, those select coaches who are able to identify, understand, and regulate their own and other's emotions, may be more effective" (Magrum & McCullick, 2019, para. 5).

Within the articles reviewed that focused on emotion and coach effectiveness, the authors suggested two primary themes that were found to enhance coach effectiveness: 1) the coach's ability to identify, understand, and manage emotions, 2) striking a balance between pushing to achieve lofty standards and recognizing when these efforts have begun to overtake and undermine other important areas.

Coach-Athlete Interaction and Emotion

Related to emotion and the interaction between a coach and an athlete, the authors' research discovered a common theme— coaches demonstrate a profound influence on an athlete's life through their interaction: "Specifically, the manner in which coaches interact with athletes has been linked to performance outcomes, training effects, psychological effects, moral development, and emotional abuse" (Magrum & McCullick, 2019, para. 21).

In general, emotions can have a significant impact on an athlete's performance, and a coach, in large part, can influence and even regulate an athlete's emotion through their interaction. So, as coaches work diligently to improve their athletes' performance, they should also focus on their own emotional interactions with those athletes and what kind of impact they are having.

Personal Experience: A Young Coach's Struggle

Many years ago, as a young coach, I was not able to manage my emotions effectively; thus, my team was not able to perform to their potential. It's one of those big regrets I have in life as I did not take full advantage of the opportunity to have a profound impact on developing young people.

I graduated from college at the age of 22 and became a head high school baseball coach at the very young age of 23. I was extremely competitive, and my sole focus was on winning, not developing young men as it should have been. My competitiveness along with my misguided focus on winning caused me to live in a constant state of stress, so much so, in fact, that I began to have very painful ulcers that would keep me up at night.

My singular focus on winning and my subsequent outbursts of frustration created a roadblock that prevented me from developing more positive relationships with my players. My inability to manage my emotions and prioritize what was most important prevented me and ultimately the team from performing at our best. I was not an effective coach, did not have impactful interactions with the players, did not invest any time in developing my emotional intelligence, and was not able to circumvent severe stress.

I share this personal story so that it may be a beacon to other coaches. Understanding the X's and O's, having a solid game plan, and even getting the most out of your practice sessions is not enough to become an elite-level coach. Your ability to understand and manage your own emotions, along with being able to understand and regulate the emotions of your athletes, can indeed help you and your athletes reach peak performance.

The Importance of Emotional Intelligence

Mayer and Salovey (1997) define emotional intelligence as an individual's ability to perceive, utilize, understand, and manage their emotions. As mentioned earlier in this chapter, emotional intelligence is critical to successful coaching and, further, to overall leadership. Goleman (1998) suggests that there are five components of emotional intelligence important for leaders: self-awareness, self-regulation, motivation, empathy, and social skills.

Let's explore each of these components in more detail:

Self-Awareness

Self-awareness is the ability to understand your moods and emotions, both in terms of their effect on you and their effect on your athletes. Highly self-aware coaches are confident, have a realistic view of their abilities, and aren't afraid to admit their mistakes (Galli, n.d.).

For example, a coach with positive self-awareness might recognize that during a game, their emotions tend to get the best of them, pushing them into behaving negatively, which actually diminishes the performance of their players. Being aware of this tendency beforehand provides the coach with an opportunity to create strategies to manage these emotions in a more beneficial manner.

Self-Regulation

Self-regulation is the ability to control or redirect disruptive impulses and moods (Galli, n.d.). Iconic coaches like John Wooden or Dean Smith exemplify this trait. While they certainly experienced emotions, they were able to control or self-regulate their emotions in the face of adversity. This model of calmness and confidence during competition provided incredible encouragement and motivation to their players.

Motivation

When we think of motivation in coaching, we often focus on motivating athletes. However, Goleman's concept centers on the motivation of the coach themselves. Galli (n.d.) wrote, "Coaches who enjoy long and successful careers have a passion for coaching that extends beyond social status and records. These coaches love the excitement of competition, and the fulfillment that comes from aiding in the personal and performance development of their athletes" (para. 7).

Empathy

Empathy goes beyond concern to literally sharing the feelings of others. Coaches who have the ability to empathize are able to build strong relationships with their athletes and have athletes who are more satisfied with their sport experience (Galli, n.d.). Listening to athletes and empathizing with their concerns could drastically improve their performance.

Social Skills

Having social skills means having the ability to build and manage relationships and to persuade others. To build social skills, a coach could attempt to get to know their athletes in ways that go beyond sports, such as in their academic and personal lives. This could be done through social gatherings with the team or even retreats.

Emotional Exhaustion in Coaching

Just as it is important to manage mental exhaustion, it is equally important to manage emotional exhaustion or fatigue. As a reminder, mental exhaustion generally refers to cognitive skills, such as thinking, memory, decision-making, and problem-solving; whereas, emotional exhaustion has to do with feelings, including the ability to identify, process, and express them (Santos-Longhurst & Raypole, 2022).

Elena Aguilar (2015), in an article published in *Education Week*, provides some strategies that can help coaches deal with their emotions:

1. Name the feelings: Give words to express what you are feeling.
2. Talk or write about feelings: This helps to let things out and prevents bottling them up.
3. Explore the feelings: Try to understand where the feelings are coming from and what might have triggered the intense ones.
4. Sit with the feelings: Don't try to change them, but become more aware of them and how they manifest from within.

5. Move your body: Exercise may help the emotions fade.

6. Sleep: Begin to prioritize sleep, trying to get at least 8 hours each night.

7. Meditate: This slows your mind down and helps you focus on what's important. [Personally, I find prayer to do wonders and prefer it over meditation].

8. Engage in something creative: This could be painting, crafts, music, woodworking, etc.

9. Connect with others: The company of others who can listen and empathize can make a big difference.

Conclusion

The emotional aspect of coaching is a critical component that is often overlooked in favor of tactical and strategic considerations. However, as we've explored in this chapter, a coach's ability to manage their own emotions and those of their athletes can be the difference between good and great coaching.

By developing emotional intelligence, coaches can create more positive and productive relationships with their athletes, leading to improved performance and a more satisfying experience for all involved. Moreover, by recognizing and addressing the potential for emotional exhaustion, coaches can maintain their own well-being and longevity in the profession.

As coaches continue to seek ways to improve their athletes' performance, it's crucial to remember that emotional competence is not just an added bonus—it's a fundamental skill that can elevate coaching to new heights. By focusing on emotional intelligence alongside tactical knowledge, coaches can truly unlock their potential to impact lives and achieve greatness in their sport.

CHAPTER TEN

The Parent and Emotional Cost

Richard Fowler

His strength is perfect when our strength is gone
He'll carry us when we can't carry on
Raised in His power, the weak become strong
His strength is perfect; His strength is perfect.
—Steven Curtis Chapman, "His Strength Is Perfect"

The journey of raising an elite athlete is not just physically demanding but emotionally taxing for parents. This chapter delves into the often-overlooked emotional aspects of parenting a high-performing young athlete, offering insights and strategies to navigate this complex terrain.

Historical Context

In the 60's, sport participation was markedly different from that of today's culture. Emotional issues affecting athletic performance were rarely addressed. The standard advice for personal trauma or performance slumps was to "suck it up" and play as though nothing was wrong. However, times have changed. Modern sports programs now recognize that positive emotions can elevate an athlete's performance, while negative emotions can hinder potential.

The Shift in Approach

While many parents now acknowledge the need to address the emotional component of their young athletes' lives, others still cling to the "old school" mentality. This chapter aims to guide caregivers who want to see their young athletes perform at their highest level, both emotionally and physically.

Presenting A Balanced View of Athletic Success

The concept of balance is crucial in athletics. *Merriam Webster's Dictionary* defines balance as "stability produced by even distribution of weight on each side of the vertical axis." For young competitors, achieving emotional balance may be the most critical aspect of their athletic journey.

Unfortunately, our culture often glorifies an imbalanced view of athletic success. Sports media and interviews with coaches and professional athletes frequently promote emotional imbalance, which can become a misguided mantra for parents. Consider these common, yet problematic, quotes:

- "There is no room for second place. The objective is to win."

- "It kills me to lose. If I'm a troublemaker—and I don't think that my temper makes me one—then it's only because I can't stand losing. That is the way I am about winning. All I ever want to do is finish first."

- "I take the game seriously. That is why I demand so much of my players. You have to win—everything, all the time. What is sleeping and eating when compared to winning?"

While these quotes don't represent the entirety of attitudes toward sports, they reflect a pervasive and potentially harmful view. Winning and self-sacrifice for elite athletic status are only beneficial when balanced with an athlete's other life roles.

Parents' Role in Shaping Values

Caregivers must recognize that sports participation can affect a child's values, both positively and negatively. Parents are best positioned to guide young athletes through their sports experiences, helping them reap lifelong mental, emotional, and spiritual benefits. Through thoughtful engagement and consistent reinforcement of core values, parents can help their children develop positive traits like perseverance, teamwork, and integrity. The way parents frame victories, losses, and daily challenges in sports can profoundly impact how their children approach not just athletics, but all of life's future endeavors.

The "Helicopter Parent" Phenomenon

Many parents, out of love and concern, may adopt a "helicopter parent" approach, making all decisions for their young athletes to prevent future regrets. However, this can lead to problematic dynamics:

The Parent's Approach	The Athlete's Response
It is okay to push problems "under the rug."	To survive I must deny or ignore existing problems.
Feelings are not to be expressed openly.	Tight lips will avoid conflict but win approval.
Worth is tied to giving 110% at all times.	Anything but perfection indicates failure.
Do as I say, not as I do.	Subtle retaliation gets results.
Typical age-appropriate play is not okay.	This is serious business; play is for kids.
The parent is the child's "savior."	If I try harder, I will be approved.

When adults assume a controller-dictator role, athletes may become emotionally dependent, believing that survival in the system requires mute submission, sacrifice, commitment, and dedication. True success for elite athletes is enhanced when they develop responsible decision-making processes.

Implementing the 1-4-16 Formula with Aspiring Elite Athletes

The 1-4-16 formula (Fowler & Ford, 2021, pp. 61-66) can help caregivers and student-athletes feel emotionally comfortable in their respective roles at home. This formula categorizes family rules into three tiers:

1. **Absolutes**: Core values that cannot be broken
2. **House Rules**: Observable derivatives of core values maintained for family harmony
3. **Preferences**: Areas where children and teens are allowed self-expression and self-monitoring

The formula suggests that for each single absolute, there should be about four house rules, which then yield sixteen areas of preference. This approach allows children and teens to learn self-reliance and self-monitoring. See the following examples:

1. Household example:

   Absolute: "Responsibility" - Every family member must be responsible for the upkeep and well-being of the home.

   House Rule: On Monday, the teen is assigned to mow the grass by Saturday because guests will be at their home on Saturday evening.

   Preference: The teen can choose when to mow the grass, as long as it's completed by Saturday noon.

2. Athletic example:

   Absolute: "Commitment"—If participating in a sport, the athlete must commit to that team.

   House Rule: Before signing up for a team, the athlete and caregivers must make a pro-and-con list. If participation is agreed upon, a contract is signed by both the athlete and parent.

Preference: Before signing the contract, the student athlete can share their view on the proposed commitment and has the right to veto parental wishes.

Caution: Avoid reversing the formula by issuing 16 absolutes for every 1 preference, as this will deflate motivation, morale, and enthusiasm.

Caregivers Need to Practice What They Preach

While perfect parenting doesn't exist, caregivers must strive to be the best role models for their aspiring young athletes. Values are more likely caught than taught, and inconsistencies between words and actions can lead to emotionally confused and stressed athletes.

Defining "Parent Wounds"

Bob Record, in his book, *Ending the Cycle of Father Wounds* (2020, pp. 8-14), defines a parent wound as "an emotional injury to the heart and soul caused by what a caregiver did—or did not do—in words, actions or inactions as a child grew through childhood and adolescence, damaging or rupturing relationships as a result."

These wounds, if left unattended, can deepen and become more infected, requiring time to heal. For athletes, these wounds are like emotional leg weights, hindering their ability to perform at their full potential.

Case Study

A professional NBA player sought counseling to deal with his family of origin. He noticed his performance decline when his parents were in the stands watching him play. It became apparent that his father was trying to live vicariously through his son, even blaming the player's marriage and children for subpar game performances. This athlete admitted that his father's words and attitudes haunted him continually, nearly driving him to quit the game. Extensive counseling was required to help him change his worldview and move past these wounds.

Understanding That Emotional Health Is Enhanced by a Proper View of Competition

Competition, while not unique to sports, plays a crucial role in shaping a youngster's values. Values are determined by the cognitive, left side of the brain but are solidified in the emotional, right side. Thus, greater emotional maturity leads to more positive outcomes in sports.

Unfortunately, some parents and coaches lead youngsters to believe that individual pride and achievement are the primary goals of competition. This philosophy can damage an athlete's self-esteem, creating the belief that "When I win, I am a great person, and when I lose, I am a nobody."

As noted by C. S. Lewis in *Mere Christianity*, a healthier approach recognizes that "Pride, by its very nature, requires competition to exist, but that competition can exist without pride" (1980, pp. 209-210). Athletes should be encouraged to compete against themselves rather than constantly comparing themselves to others. As President Theodore Roosevelt wisely said, "Comparison is the thief of joy."

Teaching the Elite Athlete the Difference Between "Excellence" and "Perfectionism"

The Bible suggests that satisfaction comes from doing one's best. Galatians 6:4 states, "Let everyone be sure that he is doing his very best, for then he will have the personal satisfaction of work well done, and won't need to compare himself with someone else" (Living Bible, 1971).

Many athletes are robbed of elite status because they're taught that *excellence* and *perfectionism* are identical when, in reality, they are not. *Excellence* is based on incremental goals an athlete strives to achieve and the athlete's willingness to pay the price to reach those goals. It's relative to an athlete's current level of expertise. *Perfectionism* demands the highest level of performance from the outset, regardless of an athlete's current capabilities.

Parents and coaches should encourage athletes to do the following: 1) give their best effort during every available minute in practice, 2) pour themselves wholeheartedly into their sport during play, and 3) use all available resources, including studying their sport and training both mind and body.

Caregivers Need to Keep up to Date on the Emotional Well-Being of Their Young Athletes

Recent studies highlight the increasing importance of addressing athletes' emotional well-being. An NCAA survey (2020) found a 150-200% increase in mental health concerns among college athletes in the last two years. Despite this, only 10% of emotionally struggling college athletes reach out for help, according to Athletes for Hope (Reeves, 2021). Factors contributing to this reluctance may include the following:

- Stigma against counseling
- Lack of mental health resources
- Cultural norms that teach athletes to ignore their emotional lives

As Bryan Armstead, CEO of Apollo Sports Counseling, notes, "Athletes are not going to reveal their problems because in sports they are taught to be tough and hard. Athletes are taught not to show emotion unless you're winning games" (Armstead, 2021).

Conclusion

For caregivers raising elite athletes in this generation, it's crucial to erase the stigma against seeking help for emotional issues. Parents must be as aware of their children's emotional state as they are of their grades and performance stats. By addressing the emotional aspects of athletic development, parents can help their young athletes achieve true excellence, both on and off the field.

CHAPTER ELEVEN

The Parent and Monetary Cost

Stacy Hall

"But don't begin until you count the cost. For who would begin construction of a building without first calculating the cost to see if there is enough money to finish it? 29 Otherwise, you might complete only the foundation before running out of money, and then everyone would laugh at you. 30 They would say, 'There's the person who started that building and couldn't afford to finish it!'
—Luke 14:28-30

As parents, we love our children and are willing to sacrifice everything for them to achieve their goals and happiness. But at what cost? It can be difficult at times to determine what is best for our aspiring elite athletes while balancing the needs of the rest of our family. Not many of us have unlimited time and financial resources that we can devote to helping our children develop into elite-level athletes. And even once they do compete at an elite level, how long can we sustain the financial responsibilities that come with it? And what exactly is the goal? A college scholarship, a professional contract, riches, fame, self-actualization? What's the point?

I have worked in the sports industry for nearly 30 years as a coach, administrator, and college athletic director. My wife and I have also raised two kids of our own (one of which is an NCAA Division I athlete) and have served as a host family for two international students who both played college basketball. During this time, we have met with many, many parents who have struggled to figure out the appropriate financial investment to make to put their kids in the best possible position to reach their goals. It's not an easy decision.

Realism and Elite Status

My experience has taught me several things that I think are valuable and worth sharing. First, you must be realistic about their "elite" status. Talent alone is not the sole indicator of becoming an elite athlete. Desire, work ethic, commitment, coachability, and sometimes financial ability can all have a major impact on a young athlete's ability to become (and maintain being) an elite-level athlete.

A brief personal example includes my daughter and my youngest son. My youngest son is 17 at the time of this writing. He's played several sports growing up but primarily focused on basketball. He is hands down one of the best naturally gifted athletes that I've ever seen. Strength, speed, hand-eye coordination, grit, toughness, balance, endurance, all of it—he's got it. But he never had the desire to commit to honing his craft, which is perfectly acceptable. He decided to invest his time in other areas that brought him more happiness. Conversely, my daughter has a baseline of talent but admittedly is not one of the most naturally talented golfers. However, she has become an elite-level athlete because of her tenacious work ethic and highly competitive nature. She has a strong desire to improve and is willing to do the things necessary to hone her craft.

You may have children, or know of other children, who fall into one of these characteristics. My point is this, before making the financial investment in developing an elite-level athlete, first be sure that this young person is willing and able to do the things necessary to becoming an elite-level athlete. It's possible to spend tons of money trying to help your young athlete compete at elite status, only to learn your financial contribution alone will not get it done. Piper Gilles, a Canadian Olympic Medalist Ice Dancer, said, "Money can't buy hard work, sacrifice, and dedication" (O'Connell, n.d., para. 5).

Defining the Goal

Secondly, what's the point? Before you invest possibly tens of thousands of dollars into your child's development, I suggest you answer the question, what exactly is it that I'm trying to accomplish? Does the young athlete want to play professionally? Are you trying to secure a college scholarship? If so, how much scholarship is acceptable, and at what level of college? Is obtaining an athletic scholarship more important than your "net out-of-pocket cost" for college?

Let's Talk Numbers

Ferriss (n.d.) suggests that by the age of 9 or 10, some golfers and swimmers may begin pulling away from their peers as a result of their talent and focus. She adds that by "the age of 12 or 13, all golfers and swimmers at his or her level will be talented and focused, and it will be the ones with superior training and resources–including financial resources–who pull away from that pack" (Ferriss, n.d., para. 3).

Corbin and Culp (2019) note a 2016 study that found parents reported spending between 2 to 10 percent of their family's gross annual household income on athletic activities, per child. Corbin and Culp further indicate,

> The costs of year-round training programs, travel, equipment, facility, and coaching fees have turned youth sports into a $17 billion-a-year industry, according to WinteGreen Research, a market research firm that tracks the industry. A 2016 TD Ameritrade study reported that two out of 10 families are spending $1,000 per month on elite youth sports. (Corbin & Culp, 2019, para. 5)

According to Ferris, "Not all sports carry the same price tag. Skiers can easily spend more than $40,000 per year, whereas nationally competitive soccer players may spend only $5,000 per year" (n.d., para. 7). Gigante (2022) suggests that ice hockey travel teams can cost upwards of $10,000 or more per year due to equipment, facility costs, enrollment fees, and coaching. O'Connell (n.d.) shared that Chris Chard, an associate professor at Brock University's sport management program estimated that players who want to train at an elite level can easily spend up to $15,000 per year depending on the sport, and that is for only one child. Chard went on to say that his sons can go through 3 to 4 $300 hockey sticks each season and that parents can easily face peer pressure to buy "premium" equipment (O'Connell, n.d.).

The level of equipment purchased can be a challenging question. Paul Poirier, another Canadian Olympic Ice Dancer, suggests that "the best time to invest in premium equipment is when you feel the lower-grade equipment is impeding the athlete from achieving their best and is breaking down too quickly because the athlete is training so much" (O'Connell, n.d., para. 15). This is exactly the process that we went through with my daughter and her golf clubs. We started with a basic grade starter set. Once she got older and started playing more competitive golf, we purchased her a high mid-grade set of clubs. Finally, once she began competing at Division I collegiate level, we purchased a higher-grade club to help her reach and sustain a better performance.

A high school baseball catcher could spend around $2,500 purchasing required gear such as catcher's mitts, leg guards, shoes, protective underwear, helmet, and bags, all of which need to be replaced every few years (Gigante, 2022). A 2023 report by Project Play (Youth Sports, 2023) revealed the following information related to the cost of youth sports:

- In 2022, the average youth sports parent spent $883 on one child's primary sport per season.
- Of the four major sports, parents spend more money on soccer ($1,188 average cost) and basketball ($1,002) than baseball ($714) and tackle football ($581).
- On average across all sports, parents spent more annually on travel ($260 per sport, per child) than equipment ($154), private lessons ($183), registration fees ($168), and camps ($111).

Participation in elite sports can be even more costly. A 2019 survey by Project Play revealed that families with children playing elite levels can frequently spend $12,000 per year or more on sports like lacrosse, gymnastics, ice hockey, tennis, and skiing/snowboarding and even up to $9,000 per year on less expensive sports (Gigante, 2022). Private training and summer camps can increase these costs considerably. Furthermore, it's very important to keep in mind that none of these estimates include the cost of parents missing work due to supporting their young athletes at competitions, which for some, can be a significant loss of revenue for the family.

How the Hall Family Managed Golf

To provide a real-world example of financial costs associated with developing an elite-level athlete, I have provided a conservative estimate on what a family can easily spend on the development of a young golfer beginning in the 6th grade through the summer after her 12th-grade year –7 total years. Having been intimately aware of the costs associated with competing in junior golf, I can attest that these estimates are very reasonable. It's important to note that these costs do NOT include costs associated with playing high school golf. These cost estimates are just for a competitive junior golf schedule of 8 tournaments per year (4 overnight tournaments and 4 local tournaments). Many competitive junior golfers can play considerably more tournaments in a year and sometimes even forego the high school golf season to compete in more competitive junior tours.

Expenses from 6th Grade through 12th Grade

- Three sets of clubs (starter set, mid-level, advanced set): $4,500 total
- Lessons ($75 x 12 lessons/yr. x 7 years): $6,300
- Tournament Fees (Avg. $200 tournament fee x 8 tournaments/yr. for 7 years): $11,200
- Travel for Tournaments (Hotel, Gas & Food):
- Hotel: $130 avg./night x min. of two nights = $260 x 4 tournaments/yr. x 7 yrs. = $7,280

- Gas: $100 avg. roundtrip/tournament x 8 tournaments = $800/yr. x 7 yrs.= $5,600
- Food: $100/day x min. of two days x 8 tournaments x 7 yrs. = $11,200
- Clothing/Uniforms (Min. of $500/yr. for 7 years): $3,500
- Other Equipment (shoes, golf balls, gloves, etc. – min. of $300/yr. for 7 years): $2,100
- Total 7-Year Investment: $51,680 ($7,383 per year)*
- *Note: Does not account for time that parents miss from work.

Is It Worth It? The Realities of Elite Sports: Love, Scholarships, and Professional Dreams

I think that most elite athletes would say they do it for the love of the game and because they either want to earn an athletic scholarship or they want a chance to play professionally. While these are noble aspirations, it's crucial to understand the statistical realities of these goals. Let's delve into each of these scenarios, using golf as our consistent example.

The Love of the Game

The passion for a sport is often the primary driver for young athletes. This intrinsic motivation is invaluable and can lead to lifelong benefits, regardless of professional or collegiate outcomes. However, it's important to balance this passion with realistic expectations and a well-rounded approach to personal development.

The Pursuit of Athletic Scholarships

Many young athletes and their parents view receiving athletic scholarships as the ultimate goal and justification for their investments. However, the numbers tell a sobering story. According to Scholarship Stats.com, in 2022, only 5.9% of high school male golfers and 6.4% of high school female golfers end up competing at any collegiate level. A mere 1.4% of male golfers and 1.5% of female golfers end up competing at the Division I level (Golf, n.d.). Let's put these figures into perspective:

- Out of 1,000 high school golfers, only about 60 will play in college at any level.
- Of those 1,000, only about 15 will compete at the Division I level.

It's important to note that these statistics represent those who make it onto college teams, not necessarily those who receive substantial scholarships. Many college athletes receive only partial scholarships or walk on without any athletic aid.

The Professional Dream

The odds of becoming a professional athlete are even slimmer. In golf, for example,

- The PGA Tour, the highest level of professional men's golf, has about 250 members.
- The LPGA Tour, the premier women's professional golf organization, has approximately 220 active players.

Considering that there are over 2 million high school golfers in the United States alone, the percentage who will go on to have a successful professional career is fractionally small.

Alternative Perspectives

Given these statistics, young athletes and their parents must consider the following:

- The value of education alongside athletic pursuits
- Developing transferable skills through sports that can benefit other career paths
- The importance of having a backup plan or parallel career development
- The intrinsic benefits of sports participation beyond professional or collegiate aspirations

By understanding these realities, families can make more informed decisions about investments in youth sports, balancing the pursuit of athletic excellence with overall life preparedness.

The average golf scholarship* amounts are provided below (Golf, n.d.):

Division	Men	Women
NCAA I	$18,015	$18,827
NCAA II	$6,495	$7,986
NAIA	$7,836	$7,733

*Note: The NCAA categorizes golf as an equivalency sport for scholarship purposes. This means that a partial scholarship can be awarded.

The published 2022-23 cost of attendance at the University of Georgia is $27,542 (Cost of Attendance, n.d.). In Georgia, due to our state-wide lottery program, residents who meet certain academic thresholds can earn the Hope Scholarship. This is not, however, a given. A high school student must meet a 3.0 cumulative GPA in core classes (math, science, English, social studies) among other things. At the University of Georgia, this amount is equal to $4,410 for 15 hours per semester, or $8,810 for the year (The Hope and Zell Miller Scholarships, n.d.). For this example, let's assume our college athlete qualifies for Hope. So, once we back out the $8,810 scholarship from the $27,542 total cost of attendance, we are left with $18,732 due. Based on the chart above that lists national scholarship averages, if our child is one of the very few that earns a full scholarship, we nearly break even. If our child only earns a partial scholarship, we could have to contribute a sizeable amount.

If our child attends an NCAA Division II school or NAIA level school, our out-of-pocket cost could be even more after the athletic aid is applied. If we use the total cost of attendance above, which is in alignment with most state schools, apply the Hope Scholarship, and we assume that we receive the full average athletic aid for a female in DII, our annual out-of-pocket cost is still $10,746. For NAIA it's $10,999, again, if we receive the Hope academic scholarship.

Now, as a point of comparison, what would happen if we took that $51,680 that we spent on golf between 6th and 12th grades, and instead invested in a College Savings 529 account. Scenario 1: let's assume we invest 1/7th of the amount each year for 7 years beginning in the 6th grade into an index fund earning a conservative 5% (note: the U.S. stock market has averaged nearly 10%

return annually since 1926). Our ending balance after 7 years, just before entering college, would be $70,795. This amount nearly covers the full cost of attendance after applying the Hope Scholarship. Scenario 2: if we invested 1/18th of the amount each year from birth through 12th grade in the same index fund returning 5% annually, we would earn $92,875 by the time our child was ready to enter college. This amount easily covers the total cost of attendance after Hope and covers the vast majority of it without Hope.

Alternative Investment Strategies

For parents who may not be able to afford the high costs of elite sports training, there are alternative strategies to consider:

- Local community programs and clubs that offer quality training at lower costs.
- Focusing on multi-sport participation to develop overall athleticism and reduce sport-specific expenses.
- Utilizing online resources and tutorials for skill development.
- Exploring cooperative arrangements with other families to share travel and equipment costs.

Case Studies: The Financial Journey

Sarah's Story: Sarah's parents invested heavily in her gymnastics career from age 6 to 16. While she achieved state-level success, the family's finances were strained. Her younger brother's educational opportunities were limited as a result. Sarah ultimately decided not to pursue gymnastics in college, leaving her parents with mixed feelings about their decade-long investment.

Jason's Journey: Jason's family took a measured approach to his soccer development. They balanced paid training with local club participation and focused on academic excellence. Jason earned a partial athletic scholarship to an NCAA Division II school, combined with academic scholarships, resulting in a full ride. His parents feel their strategic investment paid off both athletically and academically.

Long-Term Financial Impacts

The decision to heavily invest in a child's athletic pursuits can have far-reaching financial consequences:

- Delayed retirement savings for parents
- Reduced resources for siblings' education or extracurricular activities
- Potential debt accumulation
- Opportunity costs of time and money that could have been invested elsewhere

It's crucial for families to consider these long-term impacts when making decisions about athletic investments.

Psychological Effects of Financial Investment

The significant financial investment in a child's athletic pursuits can create unintended psychological pressures:

- Increased performance anxiety due to perceived need to "justify" the investment
- Potential resentment from siblings who may feel neglected
- Difficulty transitioning away from the sport if the child loses interest or doesn't achieve elite status
- Parental stress and potential marital strain due to financial pressures

Open communication and regular check-ins with all family members are essential to address these potential issues.

Financial Planning Resources

For families navigating the complex financial landscape of elite youth sports, several resources are available:

- Sports-specific financial advisors who understand the unique challenges of athletic families
- Online calculators to project long-term costs and savings strategies

- Workshops and seminars offered by youth sports organizations on financial planning
- Books and podcasts dedicated to the financial aspects of youth sports

Utilizing these resources can help families make more informed decisions about their athletic investments.

Conclusion

I love sports. I cannot imagine my life without sports, and I'm thrilled that all of my children embrace the sport(s) that they are passionate about. Basketball scholarships have, indeed, paid for two of our international children to get through college and we are grateful. Sports have also taught our children very important life lessons and skills, such as time management, commitment, teamwork, work ethic, delayed gratification, leadership, grit, emotional control, respect for others, sportsmanship, camaraderie, etc. Sports can also fill our hearts with joy and leave long-lasting happy memories.

I say all that to underscore that even though there is indeed a financial cost, and at times, a hefty financial cost, there doesn't have to be any more required return on your investment than what I've already listed. However, if you are looking for a financial return on your investment in elite sports, it's important to 1) be realistic about what is obtainable, 2) be clear on what you are trying to accomplish, and 3) be aware of other ways to accomplish that same goal. Having these answers can help lead you to the best course of action. The purpose of this chapter is to prepare you for some of the costs that you might incur along your journey and to challenge you to ask the question at each new step, "Is it worth it?" This is a decision that you and your young athlete will need to make together.

By expanding on these aspects, we provide a more comprehensive view of the financial landscape parents must navigate when supporting an elite young athlete, while maintaining the personal and insightful tone of the original text.

CHAPTER TWELVE

Final Tips for Parents of Athletes

Richard Fowler, Stacy Hall, and Holly Haynes

Direct your children onto the right path,
and when they are older, they will not leave it.
—Proverbs 22:6 (NLT)

1. Make sure you, as parents, don't live your lives through your children. So often, parents project onto their children the need to have athletic success they didn't have when they were young.

2. Don't continue to tell your young athlete that he or she is the best! As the competition becomes more strenuous, in a majority of cases, your child will not be the Michael Jordan of his/her sport.

3. As the competition increases, your child may be on par with his/her peers talent-wise; however, being more intrinsically than extrinsically motivated makes an athlete stand out over peers. As parents, observe your child's reaction to practicing on his/her own when "more fun social events" are occurring simultaneously. Does your child beg to go

outside to hone his/her skills when no one else is around to participate? "Passion" and forgoing other interests to better oneself for a sport is tied to intrinsic motivation.

4. If you as parents see your young athlete's passion waning, it is usually a result of two basic factors: (a) interest in the sport has subsided, or (b) too much pressure has been placed on the child. In most cases it is the latter.

5. Due to club sports, many young athletes reach burn-out early in their career. *The Washington Post* reported that by the age of 13, 70% of youth sports participants have dropped out of competitive competition. Kids need to be kids. Up through 6th grade, children ought to have a multitude of athletic options to choose from. From 7th-9th grades, children ought to have their athletic choices narrowed down to two. And, after careful evaluation of talent and skill sets, if the child is deemed to be a standout, then when entering high school, the focus can be only on one sport.

6. The definition of "burn-out" is "those you love or activities you love start to become your enemy." Communicate with your young athlete what you are observing if you begin to see a decline of interest in the sport. Getting to the root cause might create renewed interest.

7. Don't discuss player mistakes on the way home from the game.

8. Don't act like little kids when in the stands watching your child play. Be an adult. Children roleplay what they see their parents do!

9. Emphasize to your young athlete that character development and rising above adversity is a positive virtue to strive for. Skill progression is more important than "winning at all costs."

10. Understand that in today's culture social media will almost trump the importance of sports. Years ago, before social media, sport activity was a way to fill up the day. Today, social media will fill up over eight hours a day in our young generation. Thus, in many cases the quality of performance decreases.

11. Unfortunately, coaches and parents consciously or unconsciously lead youngsters to believe that individual pride and achievement are the most important goals in athletics. Ego then becomes the motivating force for performance rather than commitment to the team.

12. Speaking of egos, a parent who puts their young athlete on the pedestal of perceived greatness, will teach that child to become narcissistic. Narcissism has been a major reason why many potentially great athletes fail. On the flip side, commitment to the team more than self can lead to a humble spirit.

13. As a parent/teacher of your young athlete, instill in them the three-part formula for personal success:

    1) First, emphasize that your young athlete gives his/her best effort during every minute available in practice. This means not letting up during unusually tough drills, being prompt, and disciplining oneself to practice.

    2) Second, after preparing thoroughly with a positive mental attitude, the athlete now can confidently give all—physically, mentally, and emotionally—to his/her performance. To drain oneself in competition may be the best description of this second phase.

    3) Third, an athlete should use all resources available, should study the sport, using brain power as well as brawn power to better him/herself in the sport.

14. Teach your young athlete to compete against self, rather than focusing on the opponent. For example, if a basketball player averages 7 points and 3 rebounds a game, the focus when in a game ought to be, "l am striving for 9 points and 4 rebounds tonight" rather than "l must beat my opponent."

15. Parents, teach your young athletes to have fun while playing their sports. Once a sport becomes a job, many athletes lose personal motivation to continue at a high level of play.

16. Unless there are dire circumstances involved, tell your young athlete he/she must stick the season out, even if the

coach is not playing your child as much as he/she deserves. By doing this you are teaching the virtues of loyalty and commitment to the team.

17. Parents, do your homework concerning signing up your child to a prospective team or coach BEFORE committing your young athlete to a team. Once you are satisfied with your choice, treat coaches as an equal, not as inferior to you. Respect them and let them coach, even if their decisions seem not to be in your favor.

18. If a child athlete complains about the team or coach, don't immediately agree with that child, rather ask him or her what they can do to change the situation and make a distinct action plan. Learning this skill will prepare them for future bumps in the road of life.

19. Make sure the youth sport organization serves the best interest of the athlete and not the parents.

20. Before a season, ask your young athlete the degree of involvement they want from you, the parents, in discussing their performance, etc. Honor their wishes as much as possible.

21. As parents, remember your love for the young athlete should not be based on successful performance. Parents should affirm their love for their child prior to and after a game.

22. Keep in mind that overbearing parents are toxic to their children who play sports.

23. Parents need to remember that we learn not only from success but also from failure. If a child plays poorly in one game, instead of overcoddling him/her, discuss what can be learned from the game and develop a strategy to correct bad habits. Overcoddling a child after a poor performance subconsciously encourages him/her not to be solution oriented.

24. Young athletes who are afraid to make a mistake for fear of a reprimand from a parent yelling at them in the stands will tighten up and cannot play relaxed. Also, this fear will keep athletes from taking risks that can improve their game.

25. If a young athlete cries after a defeat, it may be a result of a broken competitive spirit. But more often than not, crying after a defeat is the result of perceived parental rejection when he/she gets home.

26. Prior to a season, parents should rehearse the boundaries for the upcoming season. State things like, "By signing up for this season you are committed to finish the season, attend practices, etc." Parents should have the young athlete repeat back to them what was agreed on. This teaches the child to take ownership of his/her decisions.

27. It has been said that "What doesn't kill you makes you stronger. Fortune favors those who dare." Parents, let your young athletes struggle through conflict or misfortunes so that they may grow stronger.

28. Parents need to let the natural consequences occur, rather than try to continually run interference for their young athletes. Parents should not have to remind them, "Don't forget to take your glove to practice," "Remember, practice is today at 3," etc. Allowing children to miss a practice or forget a glove is a good way to teach responsibility. Many children become mentally lazy and rely on parents to be their calendar.

29. Don't smother your young athlete. Doing so will keep your child from maturing to the next level of social and psychological development.

30. Don't use rewards to honor a young athlete who hit a home run to win the game ("Son, I want to treat you to an ice cream cone because you played so well") but refuse to offer the ice cream cone to the child who just lost the game by striking out. To do so is to send the message that love is conditional.

31. When talking to their young athletes, parents ought to focus more on the pluses and minuses of their child's performance and discuss ways to improve over discussing the wins and losses of the team.

32. To raise healthy children, parents need to treat the non-athlete child the same as the athlete child. This prevents an inferiority complex from developing in the child who does

not participate in sports. This inferiority complex and resentment can develop when every weekend the non-athlete must attend big brothers' soccer game.

33. Parents, don't coach from the sidelines.

34. On the way home from a game, parents should only focus on the child, rather than on game stats: "It was my pleasure to see my daughter out there on the field playing. That brings great joy to me. It's fun for me to see you perform."

35. Parents ought not to glamorize the talent of their young athlete by saying something like, "Son, it's going to be great to see you play pro ball someday." This kind of language will only produce fantasy expectations that most likely will never materialize.

36. Parents, don't be resentful if you spend ten years and mega money on your young athlete to play select sports only to find out that at the end of that ten years the athlete no longer wants to compete. To become resentful is to say to your child, "Look at all I have done for you, and you don't appreciate me for the sacrifices I have made on your behalf." The end result will yield psychological wounds that may never be healed.

37. Parents are not always the best ones to mentor their young athletes in fine tuning their skills. Besides the team's coach, having a knowledgeable mentor often yields more success.

38. If parents instill in their young athlete that their love is unconditional rather than based on performance, the athlete will be able to deal with an injury in a healthier manner.

39. The old saying "No pain, no gain" is a good teaching tool for parents. It is understandable that a major illness or a severely pulled muscle will cause the athlete to be sidelined for a time. However, many minor injuries are treated by parents as if they were major, causing their young athlete to withdraw from competition when it was not necessary to do so. It is sad to see athletes with a minor sprain being put on crutches by their parent—when heat and ice, and an ankle wrap could be administered, and the athlete sent back on the field to play.

40. Parents, be aware of the psychological effects of hyper-competitiveness. Make sure your young athlete has a balanced life so that he/she can develop in all areas of life.

41. It has been said that "The goal of athletics isn't exclusively to excel at the game.... the goal also is to excel at being an athlete." As young athletes push themselves to a higher level, a degree of satisfaction can be experienced—a value that will follow them throughout life. Parents, remember that your gift to your children of allowing them to play a sport will positively affect their adult life in the future.

42. There is a saying that goes like this: "You can lead a horse to water, but you can't make him drink." That may be true, but there is no law that prohibits one from putting out salt blocks, so when the horse licks the salt, it gets thirsty and goes to the tank for a drink! So, the moral of the story is, even though one cannot force the horse to drink, that individual did cause the horse to drink because he put out the salt blocks. Parents, when your children show an initial passion in a sport but later become distracted by outside interests, put out salt blocks for them to lick so they return to the sport with greater enthusiasm.

43. Parents should remember that most referees are not professionally trained, so give them slack! Putting up with the mistakes of a referee is part of maturity growth for your young athlete.

44. Most arguments parents have with their child's coaches stem from putting a $1,000 price tag on a 5-cent issue. Have your child wait at least 24 hours before addressing a concern to the coach.

45. Only when parents observe blatant abuse or a game getting out of hand, should they run interference on behalf of their child.

46. Parents ought not to use "all" or "nothing" language when talking with their young athlete. Often there is a middle ground that can be reached.

47. Parents need to teach their young athlete not to blame the weather or playing field for a poor performance. This often

allows the child to develop "acceptable excuses" for negative play.

48. If a parent exhibits poor behavior at a game, that parent needs to ask their young athlete for forgiveness. The child knows this parent is human yet is relieved when the poor behavior is addressed.

49. Many coaches will bark out to his/her players, "You must give 110%"! This however is sending the wrong message. Parents need to articulate to their young athlete that the goal is 90% perfection, leaving 10% for being human. Even in the pros, no one can achieve 100% perfection, or the unthinkable 110% which is above being human!

50. Parents need to remember that conflict at home will drastically affect the performance of their young athletes.

51. For a young athlete to maximize his/her potential, parents must be flexible.

52. Parents should spend quality and quantity time with their young athlete in scenarios apart from sport-related activities.

53. Research has shown that a good number of parents have gone from being "helicopter parents" to being "lawnmower parents." Instead of merely hovering over their young athlete, many parents in this current generation have become so intricately intertwined in the affairs of their child (called "co-dependency") that the child is unable to make mental decisions, even minor ones, without the consultation and approval of their parents.

54. Parents ultimately determine whether their child should play on a travel or select team. Psychologically, the decision ought to be made in regard to what is the ultimate best for the young athlete. Some pros include more opportunities for college scholarships and a greater intense emphasis in skill development that will enhance the performance of the athlete. Some cons parents need to consider are the sheer costs of being a part of a travel team (many parents report they spent more on select team expenditures than they would have on tuition at the college of their choice), the lack

of guaranteed playing time, and the potential loss of certain life development milestones.

55. Parents often fall into a social strata trap when their child is involved in travel team play. This can lead to parental cliques that can be transferred to the young athletes, which in turn will ultimately destroy team cohesiveness.

56. If parents hassle coaches during the season, they should expect, in most cases, a negative response from the coach. The best time to have a heart-to-heart conversation with a coach is prior to or after the season is completed.

57. If a young player is bullied by a teammate, parents should first listen, without interruption to their child. Second, parents should avoid transference—transferring a previous bullying situation they may have experienced when they were young to a situation their child is currently facing. Third, work out with the young athlete a strategy he or she can employ to rectify the bullying. And finally, if it is mandated that the parents need to report the bullying to the coach, the conversation should focus on the facts and not the emotions.

58. If a young athlete needs to be punished for breaking a house rule, it is best that parents not deny athletic participation as punishment. Rather, parents ought to take away privileges. Sport participation involves commitment to the team, and by denying participation the whole team is affected. If punishment is the right course of action for violating a house rule, a suggestion is to present two or three options and let the child choose one. This transfers the ownership of the punishment back to the child.

59. If, after tryouts, a young athlete does not make the team, the parents' role is to offer unconditional support, validate their child's feelings, discourage their child from falling into the trap of being a victim, and finally help that child find another sport or event that he/she can excel in.

60. If parents desire that their young athlete be a part of a sport team, effort should be made to get to know their child's friends and their parents.

Afterword

I find peace when I'm with You
I can trust in what You'll do
If not us, what else I choose?
Where would I be? Me without You
You keep blessing me
Keep protecting me.
--Lj the Messenger, "i knw"

As we conclude this journey through the complexities of raising and coaching elite athletes, we are profoundly grateful for the time you've invested in reading and reflecting on these pages. When we first conceived of *Counting the Cost*, we recognized that the landscape of youth sports had changed dramatically from previous generations. The financial, emotional, mental, and physical investments required to develop elite athletes have reached unprecedented levels, yet the guidance available to parents, coaches, and athletes hasn't always kept pace with these changes. These rapid changes have created new challenges for everyone involved in youth sports, from parents making difficult decisions about specialization to coaches balancing competitive success with athlete well-being.

Throughout this book, we have attempted to provide a comprehensive framework for understanding and navigating these various costs. The title *Counting the Cost* speaks to more than just the financial investments—though these are certainly substantial. It addresses the full spectrum of sacrifices and commitments required from everyone involved in the development of elite athletes. Most importantly, it acknowledges that these costs must be weighed carefully against the potential benefits and aligned with each family's values and resources.

Each of us brings a unique perspective to this work. Holly Haynes, as both an educator and parent of elite athletes, has witnessed firsthand the delicate balance between nurturing athletic talent and maintaining overall well-being. Rick Fowler's extensive experience in counseling and sports psychology has provided insights into the crucial mental and emotional aspects of athletic development. Stacy Hall's background in athletic administration and coaching has illuminated the institutional and systemic challenges facing today's elite athletes. Together, our diverse experiences have allowed us to examine these challenges from multiple angles and provide practical, tested solutions.

We have shared these diverse perspectives because we believe that success in modern athletics requires a holistic understanding of all these elements. The costs we have discussed—financial, emotional, physical, and mental—are interrelated, each affecting the others in ways that weren't always recognized in previous eras of sports development. Understanding these connections has become crucial for anyone involved in elite athletics. Our research and experience have shown that addressing these elements in isolation often leads to suboptimal outcomes for young athletes.

Looking to the future, we see both challenges and opportunities. The increasing professionalization of youth sports brings higher stakes and greater pressures but also new resources and understanding about athletic development. Social media and technology have created new pressures for young athletes but also unprecedented opportunities for learning and connection. The mental health challenges we've discussed are more prevalent than ever, but so too is our understanding of how to address them and support young athletes effectively.

Our greatest hope is that this book serves as more than just a guide—we want it to be a conversation starter. The discussions about costs, values, and priorities in youth sports must happen more openly and frequently. Whether you are a parent considering the travel team route, a coach building a program, or an athlete dreaming of reaching elite status, we hope these pages have provided frameworks for making informed decisions and having productive conversations about the journey ahead. These conversations become especially crucial as the investment required for elite athletics grows.

We also hope we have emphasized that while the costs of developing elite athletes are significant, they need not be overwhelming. With proper planning, support, and perspective, these investments can yield returns that go far beyond athletic achievement. The life skills, character development, and personal growth that come from properly managed athletic pursuits are invaluable. Most importantly, we believe that understanding and accepting these costs upfront allows families to make more informed decisions about their athletic journey.

Our spiritual worldview fundamentally shapes how we view athletic development and success. The timeless principles of humility, integrity, and diligent work provide a strong foundation for elite athletes navigating the pressures of high-level competition. When athletes understand that their worth extends beyond their athletic achievements, they can pursue excellence while maintaining a healthy perspective about their sport's role in their lives. These core values help athletes balance their competitive drive with personal growth, recognizing that true success encompasses more than just athletic accomplishments. Most importantly, this foundation of values enables athletes to remain grounded even as they reach the highest levels of their sport.

To the parents reading this: We understand the weight of the decisions you face. Every choice about training, travel, specialization, and investment carries both opportunities and trade-offs. We hope this book has provided tools to help you make these decisions with greater confidence and clarity. Remember that each family's journey is unique; what works for one athlete may not work for another, even within the same family.

To the coaches: Your role has never been more challenging or more important. The best practices and insights we have shared are meant to support you in navigating the increasing complexities of developing young athletes while maintaining their well-being. The pressure to produce results must be balanced with the responsibility to nurture well-rounded individuals. Your influence extends far beyond the playing field, shaping not just athletes but future leaders and citizens.

To the athletes: Your journey is unique, and while the path to elite status is demanding, it need not come at the cost of your joy, health, or personal development. We hope this book helps you pursue your dreams while maintaining a healthy perspective on the role of sports in your life. Remember that your worth extends far beyond your athletic achievements. The lessons you learn through sports—perseverance, teamwork, resilience—will serve you well throughout your life.

As we look to the future, we believe that understanding and properly managing these various costs will become even more crucial. The landscape of youth sports will continue to evolve, but the fundamental principles we have discussed—the importance of balance, the need for proper support systems, the value of long-term perspective—will remain constant. Our commitment to advancing the conversation about healthy athletic development remains unwavering. We look forward to seeing how future generations of athletes, parents, and coaches build upon these insights to create even better pathways for athletic development.

We are deeply grateful for the opportunity to share these insights with you, and we remain committed to advancing the dialogue about healthy athletic development. Your dedication to understanding and navigating these challenges reflects the care and thoughtfulness needed in youth sports today. We hope this book becomes a valuable resource that you return to throughout your athletic journey. Most importantly, we hope it helps you find joy and purpose in the pursuit of athletic excellence.

With deepest appreciation,
Richard Fowler, Stacy Hall, and Holly Haynes

References

Chapter 2

Chow, J. Y., Shuttleworth, R., Davids, K., & Araújo, D. (2019). Ecological dynamics and transfer from practice to performance in sport. *Skill acquisition in sport*, 330-344.

Epstein, D. (2014). *The sports gene: Inside the science of extraordinary athletic performance.* Portfolio.

Ericsson, K. A., & Harwell, K. W. (2019). Deliberate practice and proposed limits on the effects of practice on the acquisition of expert performance: Why the original definition matters and recommendations for future research. *Frontiers in psychology, 10*, 2396.

Ericsson, K. A., Krampe, R. T., & Tesch-Römer, C. (1993). The role of deliberate practice in the acquisition of expert performance. *Psychological review, 100*(3), 363.

Galatti, L. R., Marques, R. F., Barros, C. E., Montero Seoane, A., & Rodrigues Paes, R. (2019). Excellence in women basketball: Sport career development of world champions and Olympic medalists Brazilian athletes. *Journal of Sport Psychology, 28*(3), 17-23.

Gladwell, M. (2008). *Outliers: The story of success.* Random House.

Ko, J. H. (2021). Replantations and the 10 000-Hour Rule—When Practice Does Not Make Perfect. *JAMA network open, 4*(10), e2129999-e2129999.

Menting, S. G. P., Hendry, D. T., Schiphof-Godart, L., Elferink-Gemser, M. T., & Hettinga, F. J. (2019). Optimal development of youth athletes toward elite athletic performance: How to coach their motivation, plan exercise training, and pace the race. *Frontiers in Sports and Active Living 1*, Article 14:1-8.

Roca, A., & Ford, P. R. (2021). Developmental activities in the acquisition of creativity in soccer players. *Thinking Skills and Creativity*, *41*, 100850.

Williams, M. & Wigmore, T. (2020). *The best: How elite athletes are made.*

Woods, C. T., McKeown, I., O'Sullivan, M., Robertson, S., & Davids, K. (2020). Theory to practice: Performance preparation models in contemporary high-level sport guided by an ecological dynamics framework. *Sports Medicine-Open*, *6*(1), 1-11.

Chapter 3

Cammarota, T., (2016). *Five ways to exasperate kids in sports*. https://playingforglory.com/2016/02/10/5-ways-toexasperate-kids-in-sports/

Dennehy, C. (2021, May 4). Two British runners scored big wins with cross-training. Here's what they can teach us. *Runner's World*. Retrieved January 8, 2023 from https://www.runnersworld.com/training/a36301124/two-british-runners-used-cross-training-for-wins/

Fitzgerald, J. (2012). *Defining athleticism: The 5 components of fitness*. Strength Running. https://strengthrunning/com/2012/10/5-components-of-fitness/.

Griffin, G., (2016). Can intuition be taught or learned? https://www.gusgriffin.net/blog/cann-intuition-be-taught--or -or-learned/.

Han, J., Waddington, G., Anson, J., & Adams, R. (2015, January). Level of competitive success achieved by elite athletics and multi-joint proprioceptive ability. *Journal of Science and Medicine in Sport*, *18*(1): 77-81. https://doi.org/10.1016/j.sams.2013.11.013

Hanson B. (2022). *Improve athlete resilience: 6 tips for coaches*. Athlete Assessments. https://www.athleteassessments.com/improve-athleteassessments.com/improve-athlete-resiliency-6-tips-for-coaches.

Hutson, M. (2019). 8 truths about intuition: What to know about what you don't know you know. *Psychology Today*.

https://psychologytoday.com/us/articles/201912/8-truths-about-intuition.

The invention of the Post-it Note. (2022). National Inventors Hall of Fame. https://www.invent.org/blog/trends-stem/who-invented-post-it-notes.

Krause, P. (2009). The benefits of cross-training. *Journal of the American Medical Athletic Association, 22*(2), 9-16.

McCauley, J. (2022). *Emboldened athletes push back on old-school coaching methods.* https://www.aol.com/news/emboldened-athletes-push-back-old-school-coaching-methods.

McClusky, M. (2014). *Faster, higher, stronger: how sports science is creating a new generation of superathletes, and what we can learn from them.* Avery.

Merriam-Webster. (2009). *Merriam-Webster collegiate dictionary*, 11th ed.

Neal, T. (2016, April 19) *Burnout in athletes.* National Athletic Trainers' Association. Retrieved January 8, 2023, from https://www.nata.org/blog/beth-sitzler/burnout-athletes.

O'Sullivan, J. (2022). *3 ways coaches can inspire their athletes*. Coaches Toolbox. https://ww.coachestoolbox.net/motivation/3-ways-coaches-can-inspire-their-athletes.

Poirier-Leroy, O. (2022). *How swimmers can develop world-class resilience*. Your Swim Book. https://www.yourswim-log.com/develop-resilence/.

Raedeke, T. D., Lunney, K., & Venables, K. (2002). Understanding athlete burnout: Coach perspectives. *Journal of Sport Behavior, 25*(2), 181-206.

Ryrie, C., ed. (1977). The New American Standard Bible (NASB), Moody Publishers.

Scott, G., (2004). Can creativity be taught? Here's what the research says. *Creativity Research Journal, 16*(4), 361-388.

6 Sports superstars who cross-train in martial arts [videos]. (2023). Evolve Daily. Retrieved January 8, 2023 from https://evolve-mma.com/blog/6-sports-superstars-who-cross-train-in-martial-arts/

Tönnies, F. (2001). *Community and Civil Society* (J. Harris, ed.), Cambridge University Press.

Tyndall, A. (2020) *10 ways to train smarter, not harder*. Athletic Evolution Sports Performance Training. https://athleticevolutionspt.com/train-smarter-not-harder/

Wilson, E., (2017). Intuition and Creativity. https://j-dm.org/archives/4029.

Chapter 4

Ariza-Vargas, L., López-Bedoya, J., Domínguez-Escribano, M., & Vernetta-Santana, M. (2011). The effect of anxiety on the ability to learn gymnastics skills. *The Sport Psychologist*, *25*(2), 127-143. https://doi.org/10.1123/tsp.25.2.127

Caine, D., Caine, C., & Maffulli, N. (2006). Incidence and distribution of Pediatric Sport-related injuries. *Clinical Journal of Sport Medicine*, *16*(6), 500-513. https://doi.org/10.1097/01.jsm.0000251181.36582.a0

Emery, C. A. (2010). Injury prevention in pediatric sport-related injuries: A scientific approach. *British Journal of Sports Medicine*, *44*(1): 64-69. https://doi.or/10.1136/bjsm.2009.068353

Frank, R., Nixdorf, I., & Beckmann, J. (2015, April). Depression among elite athletes: Prevalence and psychological factors. *Deutschz Zeitschrift für Sportmedizin*, 1-6. https://www.germanjournalsportsmedicine.com/fileadmin/content/Englische_Artikel/Originalia_Frank_englisch.pdf

Klockare, E., Gustafsson, H., Olsson, L., & Lundqvist, C. (2022). Sport Psychology Consultants' views on working with perfectionistic athletes. *Sport Psychologist*, *36*(4), 219-227. https://doi.org/10:1123/tsp.2021-0055

Main, L., & Grove, J. R. (2009). A multi-component assessment model for monitoring training distress among athletes. *European Journal of Sport Science*, *9*(4), 195-202. https://doi.org/10.1080/17461390902818260

Nicolas, M., Gaudreau, P., & Franche, V. (2011). Perception of coaching behaviors, coping, and achievement in a sport competition. *Journal of Sport & Exercise Psychology*, *33*(3), 460-468.

Rogers, T. J., & Landers, D. M. (2005). Mediating effects of peripheral vision in the life event stress/athletic injury relationship. *Journal of Sport & Exercise Psychology*, *27*(3), 271-288.

Russell, K., Christie, J., & Hagel, B. E. (2010). The effect of helmets on the risk of head injuries among skiers and snowboarders: A meta-analysis. Canadian Medical Association Journal, *182*(4), 333-340. https://doi.org/10.1503/cmaj.091080

Sabato, T., Walch, T. J., & Caine, D. J. (2016). The elite young athlete: Strategies to ensure physical and emotional health. *Open Access Journal of Sport Medicine*, *7*, 99-113, https://doi.org/10.2147/OAJSM.S96821

Winsley, R., & Matos, N. (2011). Overtraining and elite young athletes. *Medicine & Sport Science*, *56*, 97-105. https://doi.org/10.1159/000320636

Chapter 5

Blankert, T., & Hamstra, M. R. (2017). Imagining success: Multiple achievement goals and their effectiveness imagery. *Basic and Applied Social Psychology*, *39*(1): 60-67, https://doi.org/10.1080/01973533.2016,1255947

Cohn, P. (2018, December 24). *Developing mental toughness for sports.* Peak Performance Sports, Inc. https://www.peaksports.com

Dweck, C. S. (2006). *Mindset: The new psychology of success.* Random house.

Kaufman, K. A., Glass, C. R., & Pineau, T. R. (2018). *Mindful sport performance enhancement: Mental training for athletes and coaches.* American Psychological Association.

Osborne, T. (1985). *More than winning: The story of Nebraska's Tom Osborne.* Thomas Nelson Publishers.

Wilson, L. (2022, April 21). *13 ways to be more coachable.* Coaches Toolbox.net https://www.coach-estoolbox.net/program-building/13ways-to-be-more-coachable

Chapter 6

Russell, S., Jenkins, D., Rynne, S., Halson, S., & Kelly, V. (2019). What is mental fatigue in elite sports? Perception from athletes and staff. *European Journal of Sport Science, 19*(6): 1-26. https://doi.org/10.1080/17461391.2019.1618397

Santos-Longhurst, A., & Raypole, C. (2022). *How to treat and prevent mental exhaustion.* Healthline. https://www.healthline.com/health/mental-exhaustion

Chapter 7

Baumrind, D. (1971). Current patterns of parental authority. *Developmental psychology, 4*(1p2), 1.

Damour, L. (2024). *The Emotional Lives of Teenagers: Raising Connected, Capable, and Compassionate Adolescents.* Ballantine Books.

Kramers, S., Thrower, S. N., Steptoe, K., & Harwood, C. G. (2023). Parental strategies for supporting children's psychosocial development within and beyond elite sport. *Journal of Applied Sport Psychology, 35*(3), 498-520.

Chapter 8

Dweck, C. S. (2006). Mindset: The new psychology of success. Random house.

Chapter 9

Galli, N. (n.d.). *Improved coaching through emotional intelligence.* Association for Applied Sports Psychology. https://appliedsportpsych.org/resources/resources-for-coaches/improved-coaching-through-emotional-intelligence/

Goleman, D. (1998). *What makes a leader?* Harvard Business Review.

Magrum, E., & McCullick, B. (2019, May 23). The role of emotion in sport coaching: A review of the literature. *The*

Sport Journal, *24*. https://thesportjournal.org/article/the-role-of-emotion-in-sport-coaching-a-review-of-the-literature/

Mayer, J. D., & Salovey, P. (1997). What is emotional intelligence? In P. Salovey & D. J. Sluyter (Eds.), *Emotional development and emotional intelligence: Educational implications* (pp. 3–34). Basic Books.

Rennicke, S. (2014). Body, mind and soul. *Fellowship of Christian Athletes*. https://www.fca.org/fca-in-action1/2014/10/31/body-mind-and-soul#:~:text=%22One%20coach%20will%20impact%20more%20young%20people%20in,on%20the%20shoulders%20of%20coaches%20around%20the%20world.

Santos-Longhurst, A., & Raypole, C. (2022). *How to treat and prevent mental exhaustion*. Healthline. https://www.healthline.com/health/mental-exhaustion

Chapter 10

Armstead, B. (2021). Decreasing the Stigma around Athlete's Mental Health. Apolospots.org.

Bresee, T. (2021, September 10). Mental health and sports: A changing landscape. The Red and Black. Redandblack.com.

Fowler, R., & Ford, N. (2021). Grace-based counseling. Moody Press.

Lewis, C. S. (1980). Mere Christianity, Harper Collins Publishers.

Merriam-Webster. (2009). Merriam Webster's collegiate dictionary (11th ed.)

NCAA. (2020). Mental Health Concerns in Student-Athletes [survey]. research@ncaa.org.

Record, F. (2020). Ending the cycle of father wounds. M & R Legacy.

Reeves, K. (2021). Athletes Struggling with their Mental Health. Athletesforhope.org.

Taylor, K., ed. (1971). The Living Bible-paraphrased. Tyndale House Publisher.

Chapter 11

Admissions & tuition. (2023). IMG Academy. https://www.imgacademy.com/boarding-school/admissions-tuition

Corbin, C., & Culp, L. (2019). *The human cost of raising youth sports to a $17 billion industry.* Fox News. https://www.foxnews.com/sports/youth-sports-17-billion-industry-human-cost

Cost of attendance. (n.d.). University of Georgia. https://osfa.uga.edu/costs/

Ferriss, L. (n.d.). *Raising an elite athlete: A financial challenge for most parents.* MomsTeam. https://www.momsteam.com/successful-parenting/parenting-elite-athletes/travel-academics-international-competition/raising-an-?page=0%2C0

Gigante, S. (2022). Cost of youth sports: Dollars and sense. *MassMutual Blog.* https://blog.massmutual.com/post/cost-of-youth-sports-dollars-and-sense

Golf. (n.d.). Scholarship Stats.com. https://scholarship-stats.com/golf

The Hope and Zell Miller scholarships. (n.d.). University of Georgia. https://osfa.uga.edu/types-of-aid/undergraduate/scholarships/hope-and-zell-miller-scholarships/

Investment calculator. (n.d.). Calculator.net. https://www.calculator.net/investment-calculator.html

O'Connell, D. (n.d.). *A run for your money: Can you afford to raise an elite athlete?* Moneytalk. https://www.moneytalkgo.com/run-for-your-money/

Youth Sports Facts Challenge. (2023). Project Play Aspen Institute. https://www.aspenprojectplay.org/youth-sports/facts/challenges

Contributors

Richard Fowler

Dr. Rick Fowler, author/co-author of fifteen books, currently serves Truett McConnell University as the lead masters-level professor of psychology/professional counseling who specializes in sport psychology. He also serves on the Athletic Administration team as the Psychological Wellness Coordinator for all university sport teams. Prior to TMU, Dr. Fowler was the head basketball coach at two universities, a sport psychology consultant to college and professional athletes, and has been a featured speaker at sports-related conferences.

Stacy Hall

Dr. Stacy Hall has spent 27 years working full-time in the sports industry at a variety of levels. His experience includes athletic administration at the collegiate level with stints at Florida State, University of Houston, and Vanderbilt University. Dr. Hall served as an executive with ISP Sports and IMG College managing multimedia rights for the Southeastern Conference, Rupp Arena, and nine member schools within the conference.

During his tenure as Director of Athletics for Truett McConnell University, each sport set new win records as a four-year institution and in student-athlete academic success. In addition, throughout his career, Stacy has donated his time to coaching a variety of youth sports, serving on a local youth sports board, and as Chairman of Habersham Fellowship of Christian Athletes.

Dr. Hall earned his BS degree from East Carolina University, an MS from Georgia Sothern University, an MBA from Truett McConnell University, and a Ph.D. from Florida State University. He and his wife, Ivy, have raised two children (one of whom is an NCAA Division I golfer) and have hosted two international students who both played NAIA basketball. Currently, Dr. Hall serves Truett McConnell University as the Vice-President for Advancement and as a professor in the School of Business.

Holly Haynes

Dr. Holly A. Haynes serves as the Executive Director of the Pillar Research Institute at The Jacob's Ladder Group, where she designs and conducts outcomes-based research on the IWBMC™ (Interpersonal Whole-Brain Model of Care®). With over two decades of experience in higher education, she previously served as the founding Dean of the Leonhard Schiemer School of Psychology & Biblical Counseling at Truett McConnell University, where she developed graduate-level counseling programs and established significant community partnerships.

Dr. Haynes earned her doctorate in Human Development and Psychology from Harvard University, where her dissertation research focused on psychological resilience and self-perception among marginalized populations. Her research interests include neurodiversity, trauma intervention, resilience, and most recently, optimizing athletic performance for individuals with attentional differences. She co-presented "Beyond the Diagnosis: Maximizing Athletic Performance in Athletes with ADHD" at the American Association of Sports Psychologists Southeast Conference and continues to investigate the intersection of neurocognitive functioning and performance optimization.

As an educator, researcher, and consultant, Dr. Haynes brings a unique interdisciplinary perspective to sports psychology, combining her background in developmental psychology, trauma-informed approaches, and evidence-based interventions to support diverse athletes. Her current work through the Pillar Research Institute offers innovative strategies for helping neurodivergent individuals—including athletes—develop personalized techniques for maximizing cognitive performance and emotional regulation.

Dr. Haynes lives with her husband and three soccer-playing children—one daughter and two sons—whose athletic pursuits give her firsthand insight into the practical applications of sports psychology principles and the unique challenges faced by young athletes and their families.

Jay McSwain

Jay McSwain is an established author and speaker respected across the country as an expert in church member assimilation.

Since founding PLACE Ministries in 1998, he has had unwavering commitment to seeing ministers, their families, church leaders, and members thrive in the areas of ministry that God has designed them to engage in!

For over thirty years, Jay has been helping people discover their unique God-given traits and abilities while helping them maximize their personal effectiveness in both life and ministry. Jay is a passionate leader who has impacted the lives of countless youth, singles, and adults as he lives out his life verse, "You find your life as you give it away" (Matthew 16:25). He has seen lives change and groups within churches experience unprecedented numeric and spiritual growth as people begin to discover what they have to give...and then give it away!

Early in his adult life, Jay helped facilitate the rapid growth of his family's development and home-building business. After leaving his family's business in 1996, he and his wife, Ginger, moved to San Francisco to partner with Golden Gate Seminary to research the school's alumni. Jay has served as both a staff member and a volunteer in churches ranging in membership size from 10 to over 9,000 members. Jay received his M.Div. from Southwestern Baptist Theological Seminary and is a graduate of the University of Georgia and a member of the 1980 National Championship Football Team. Jay has written more than ten books and numerous other resources focused on helping the church and its members. His latest book, *The Dark Sides of Personality and How to Overcome Them*, which was written with his daughter Mary, addresses how to incorporate Biblical truths to walk in the light and not to gratify desires of the flesh that can stem from personality.

Jay has served as a trustee at Golden Gate Baptist Theological Seminary and currently serves as a trustee at Anderson University. Jay has also been the chaplain for the Atlanta Braves Organization since 2011. Some of Jay's responsibilities as chaplain include speaking and leading a worship service during the baseball season each Sunday in the stadium, participating in a Bible study with executives from the Braves front office, and helping to create and lead a mentoring program with executives and college students. Jay even finds time in his busy schedule to serve on the staff of his church as the discipleship pastor.

Jay's life experiences and passion for people, along with his dynamic leadership and motivational style, offers a unique perspective in assessing the health of the church. He has developed one of the leading assimilation resource tools in the world, reaching thousands of churches and people across the country. Jay and his wife, Ginger, live in Atlanta, Georgia, and have been married for over thirty years. They have two beautiful daughters who love Jesus and love helping others.

To gain the most benefit from *Counting the Cost*, the authors created a special workbook to complement the textbook material. To order your copy, go to The Outpost, Truett McConnell University's campus bookstore found at **www.tmoutpost.org**. You may also call **(706) 865-2134**.

ASK ABOUT SPECIAL DISCOUNTS FOR BULK ORDERS!

www.ingramcontent.com/pod-product-compliance
Lightning Source LLC
Chambersburg PA
CBHW051156120626
46547CB00012B/1088

* 9 7 8 1 9 5 4 0 2 2 0 5 8 *